DaVinci's Mental Code

PALIBOR IVERSUNE

Archway Publishing books may be ordered
through booksellers or by contacting:

Archway Publishing
1663 Liberty Drive
Bloomington, IN 47403
www.archwaypublishing.com
844-669-3957

ISBN: 978-1-6657-1493-8 (sc)
ISBN: 978-1-6657-1495-2 (hc)
ISBN: 978-1-6657-1494-5 (e)

Library of Congress Control Number: 2021925417

Print information available on the last page.

Archway Publishing rev. date: 12/23/2021

CONTENTS

CHAPTER 1

Introduction (definitions)

Throughout this book a Vitruvian Man theory is brought forth concerning *Dualism*, *Sacred Geometry*, and *Hermeticism*, insofar as how these 3 philosophical approaches are proposed to relate to one another through observing the Vitruvian Man.

The theory argues that Leonardo da Vinci, within the Vitruvian Man schematic (drawing), encoded observable (or determinable) cues linked to intended messaging relating to important psychological concepts (or aspects) considered innate to/within said 3 philosophical approaches.

Said "intended messaging" is proposed to lie shrouded amidst the schematic's more renown (or more obvious) messaging that showcases perceivable patterns which exist physically; namely as within human anatomy, previously observed by the Ancient Roman architect Vitruvius (hence the honoring name of the schematic).

NOTE: that such physical patterns are considered generally much easier to perceive (or easier to agree upon) by virtue of that which exists physically is more readily discernible in comparison to that which exists non-physically [including that which exists psychologically (or mentally)—relating to the more subjective determinations associated with *Mentalism* (term defined below)—or metaphysically—relating to the more ambiguous study of *Metaphysics* (term also defined below)]

For the purposes of this book, *Mentalism* is defined as:

Attempts to study (and/or to understand) the faculty (or the ingrained ability) of how electrochemical patterns developed within a brain may practically relate to human psychology and behaviour.

For the purposes of this book, *Metaphysics* is defined as:

Attempts to study (and/or to understand) matters concerning spirituality, ultimate reason for existence, and for what may rudimentarily exist behind (or at the root of) any sort of conceptualized materialistic façade; by which the veracity of any resultant determinations is considered correlated to the measure, amount, or prevalence such determinations can be verified to also exist across/within the respective doctrines, principles, or creeds of the manifold time-tested metaphysical (or spiritual) philosophies.

For the purposes of this book, both *Dualism* and *Duality* refer to the same idea—whilst solely referred to as *Dualism* within the pages of this book—and is defined as:

That which is fundamentally associable to the fact that only a *duo of polarities* exist as per an innate set of paradoxical parameters (or outer limits)—of a counterbalancing presence, along specified spectrums of measure—NOT ONLY within our shared 3-Dimensional physical cosmos, BUT ALSO innately as per within non-physically realms of consideration.

NOTE: that this definition is not specifically referring to Rene Descartes' thesis on Dualism being of a mind-body dual dynamic

As per the above definition, such a *duo of polarities* is understood as being of opposite, opposing, or counterbalancing *polarities of force* (or such *directionalities of force*; a.k.a. such *duality of force*).

NOTE: that such *"duality of force"* (or such a *duo of polarities*) can be conceptualized to naturally exist as a *duo* of opposite, opposing, or counterbalancing such *forces* (or such *polarities of force*) that innately exist within the same "thing" (term defined below).

Within such context, the term *"forces"* can be considered synonymous with the following terms: parts; aspects;

components; physical directionality; metaphysical directionality.

For the purposes of this book, a "thing" is defined as:

Any specific thing, able to be conceptualized, that possesses such an internal/innate *duality of force.*

NOTE: that such a "thing" could be our planet Earth whilst considering that its magnetic North and South poles can be conceptualized as per such a *duo of polarities* existing within the same "thing"

Whereby a "thing", considered in such ways, could be any one of the following (but not limited to) things: Electric Charge; Atomic Mass of Elements; Wave Forms (including sine waves, ocean waves, sound waves, and light waves); Human Emotion; Mammalian Gender.

NOTE: that such concepts concerning *Dualism* are brought forth in greater detail in Chapter 7 (of this book) wherein 12 such "things" are subjected to a certain depth of review

CHAPTER 2

The Kybalion

Within this book, *Dualism* is defined similarly to how the term is defined within a book titled *The Kybalion: A Study of the Hermetic Philosophy of Ancient Egypt and Greece.*[1]

The Kybalion addresses the premise of *Dualism* within a so-called "principle of polarity" wherein, as per this Hermetic principle, it's stated (in part) "Everything is dual; everything has poles; everything has its pair of opposites".[2]

Published in 1908, *The Kybalion* seems a Hermetic handbook (of sorts) designed (in part) to directly confront and analyze various identified intricacies within *Mentalism* (term previously defined).

---

[1] Three Initiates, *The Kybalion: A Study of the Hermetic Philosophy of Ancient Egypt and Greece* (Chicago: The Yogi Publication Society, 1908).

[2] Ibid., 32.

The Kybalion may've been created and published to bring forth the teachings of the mythical Hermes Trismegistus; considered to be a Moses-like figure associated to the path for those who seek the promise of a Hermetical illumination.

Within Christian Bull's book *The Tradition of Hermes Trismegistus*, Bull describes Hermes Trismegistus as "a legendary Hellenistic figure that originated as a syncretic combination of the Greek god Hermes and the Egyptian god Thoth".[3]

If nothing else, *The Kybalion* seems a carefully crafted book issued for *utility within the modern era* (idea discussed below). It's proposed that what's spelled out within the book could potentially be used in dangerous (or harmful) ways; possibly as per psychological processes designed for the mental conditioning of human brains (consciously or otherwise) toward becoming of similar electrochemical alignment (or cerebral fellowship) to the Ancient Egyptian and Greek elitist ruling classes.

Perhaps it's appropriate here to introduce another Hermetic principle, also found within *The Kybalion*, in its so-called "principle of mentalism" wherein states "The All is Mind; the Universe is Mental."[4]

---

[3] Christian Bull, *The Tradition of Hermes Trismegistus* (Leiden and Boston: Brill Publishers, 2018), 31-96.

[4] Three Initiates, *The Kybalion: A Study of the Hermetic Philosophy of Ancient Egypt and Greece* (Chicago: The Yogi Publication Society, 1908), 26.

NOTE: that said *Kybalion* "*utility within the modern era*" is proposed to have ultimately been built upon principles and knowledge found within the ancient book *The Hermetica* (essentially considered a revered bible-like book for such seeking Hermeticists)

During the modern era, elitists who consciously endeavour within such Hermetical means and ways are proposed to do (or have done) as much typically upon ravenous sorts of quests to learn of (and to possibly cerebrally adopt) an expected (or anticipated) philosophical supremacy connected to the study and practice of particular mental (or psychological) approaches that are understood to be directly linked to those controlling-mindsets of Ancient Egyptian and Greek society; meanwhile such sorts of ancient elitist-mindsets are generally understood as having been unfazed by the practice and incorporation of slavery within their societal framework and economy.

Furthermore, such psychological conditioning (or cerebral adoption) could dangerously manifest whereby such mesmerized modern elitists could fantastically find themselves excessively romanticized by [or becoming excessively sympathetic (or apologetic) toward] the notion of idealized—or possibly even deified—internalized mental images of certain elitist characters (or such personality types) of ancient worlds who were literally slave drivers.

The ancient philosophy of *Hermeticism* is discussed in greater detail throughout this book.

CHAPTER 3

Dualism within the Vitruvian Man

Dualistic messaging (if you will) can be observed within the Vitruvian Man schematic in (at least) the 3 following specified ways:

1. between Light and Dark, as *dually observed* between the more Enlightened look of the man's Right eye contrasted against the Darker look of the man's Left eye

2. between Chaos and Order, as observed between the *duo of full-bodied positions* of the Vitruvian Man where the man's body is more Chaotically spread out in an X pose (as if jumping in spiritual expression) *dually contrasted* against the man's body while of more physical Order standing within a T pose (as if within the so-called Christ's Pose)

3. of such *dual contrast* between the *archetype geometric shapes* (term defined below) of the Equilateral Triangle—shaded in an inverted state

(or condition) surrounding the man's left eye—
and the Circle—shaded surrounding the man's
right eye in a more circular form

For the purposes of this book, an *archetype geometric
shape* refers to:

A completely symmetrical geometric shape wherein its
perimeter (or circumference) is comprised of sides (or line
segments) that are all straightedged and equal in length.

Within a means to segue into the next chapter, highlighted
here is how the 3rd preceding observation is considered
of *Sacred Geometry* (term defined in next chapter) in
perspective (or approach), within a context of *Dualism*
(term previously defined), given that the Equilateral
Triangle and the Circle are proposed of such a *duo
of polarities*—along a specified spectrum measuring
degrees of geometric dynamism—whereby no *archetype
geometric shape* has a perimeter comprised of FEWER
(in the amount of 3) equal length straightedged sides (or
line segments) than does the Equilateral Triangle (thusly
the *archetype geometric shape* of MINIMUM geometric
dynamism), whereas, antithetically (or of such aforesaid
paradoxical parameter), there exists no *archetype
geometric shape* that has a perimeter (or circumference)
comprised of MORE equal length straightedged sides
than does the Circle [as theoretically per an Infinite
(or Eternal) amount of equal length straightedged sides
comprising its circumference (or perimeter); thusly the

archetype geometric shape of the MAXIMUM geometric dynamism].

NOTE: that within the following chapter is found further discussion upon such a theoretical "Infinite (or Eternal)" premise being associated to the circumference (or perimeter) of the Circle

CHAPTER 4

Sacred Geometry

For the purposes of this book, *Sacred Geometry* is defined as:

Whereby such clear and frequent geometric pattern is identified as naturally existing (or occurring) within the cosmos (mainly concerning within our discernible world) that a certain belief develops wherein as much is argued ultimately associable to a Creator's will, force, or program, as per universal design.

"God arithmetizes" is a Carl Friedrich Gauss quote from a book titled *The Shaping of Arithmetic*.[5] Gauss was an exceptional German Mathematician of the late Early Modern era. This quote was included to highlight the fact that such *Sacred Geometric* lines-of-thinking have long been involved within certain keen efforts of *Metaphysics* (term previously defined); while Plato's documented *Sacred Geometrical* musings date such

[5] Catherine Goldstein, Joachim Schwermer, and Norbert Schappcher, *The Shaping of Arithmetic* (Berlin Heidelberg: Springer-Verlag, 2007), 235.

philosophical approach at least as far back as to within Ancient Greece.

While acknowledging that the Circle is ALMOST ALWAYS conceptualized as having a circumference comprised of ZERO equal length straightedged sides (or line segments), it is proposed as also viable to consider that the circumference (or perimeter) of the Circle is comprised of an INFINITE number of equal length straightedged sides given the following reasoning:

The Equilateral Triangle becomes the Square upon gaining one additional equal length straightedged side. The Pentagon then forms upon gaining another such side beyond that of the Square. And as this process continues—by which *archetype geometric shapes* incrementally gain an additional equal length side—upon gaining 5 additional such sides (added to the original 3 of the Equilateral Triangle), then the Octagon visually begins to resemble quite a circularized shape [albeit of only 8 such line segments (or sides)]. Then, inevitably, this process incrementally proceeds toward a theoretical point (or premise) where an INFINITE number of equal length line segments can be conceptualized to comprise the circumference (or perimeter) of the Circle; being a conceptualized point where one additional equal length line segment can always be added, no matter how infinitesimally short (or small) such an additional side is imagined to be.

The above proposed *Sacred Geometric* analysis deals with 2D *archetype geometric shapes* whereas similar analysis of such 3D shapes can be found within the concept of *Platonic Solids*. Therein the Tetrahedron (being the 3D equivalent of the Equilateral Triangle) gives the impression of progressively (or gradually) 'popping out' (in a 3D-manner of speaking) upon the continued (or increasing) incremental incorporation of additional faces (to such a transforming shape) along its march towards inevitably morphing into the Sphere (being the 3D equivalent of the Circle).

NOTE: that whereby all such "faces" (to such a shape) are constructed of equal length line segments

As per this pathed spectrum (or sort of mathematical procession) for such a transforming (or morphing) 3D *archetype geometric shape*, the incremental gaining of (or such progressive 'popping out' into) higher degrees of geometric dynamism (within its shape) is so that by the time the shape has transitioned from the four-faced Tetrahedron into the twenty-faced Icosahedron is basically when such a 3D shape begins to offer a more Spherical impression in comparison with any previous shape along such a geometric spectrum of measure (thereby echoing of the Octagon's circularized foreshadowing within the related 2D analysis).

NOTE: that the Wikipedia webpage titled *Platonic Solids* can offer a good visual representation of the above narrative

Within Chapter 7 of this book, further discussion is found upon the premise of how an opposite, opposing, or counterbalancing *dual nature* (or such a *duality of force*, as previously discussed) can simultaneously exist within the "thing" of *archetype geometric shapes* (terms previously defined).

However, before this chapter ends, here reinforced is the paradoxical concept by which the Equilateral Triangle and the Circle respectively reside at contrasting (or antithetical) poles upon a spectrum of geometric dynamism—of a degree of geometric dynamism measured (or indicated) by the amount of equal length straightedged sides (or line segments) incorporated within its perimeter (or circumference).

CHAPTER 5

The Theory

The theory presented and detailed throughout this book ultimately works to explain why ONLY the *Vitruvian Man's head was drawn to tilt towards the right half of the large circle within the Vitruvian Man schematic*, which is explicitly determinable once the large circle has been dissected—vertically down its centreline—into a *duo* of equal-sized halves (or hemispheres).

The statement "ONLY the *Vitruvian Man's head was drawn to tilt towards the right half of the large circle within the Vitruvian Man schematic*" implies that no other part of Vitruvian Man's body is observed to noticeably tilt toward either half of the large circle. This means the torso, the pelvis, the hips, and so forth are NOT materially observed to tilt toward either half of the large circle once it has been vertically dissected into a *duo* of equal-sized portions.

Also observed is the fact that the Left eye of the Vitruvian Man was drawn to look (or appear) much Darker than his Right eye (where the Right eye seems to have a more Enlightened look).

Furthermore, observed is the fact that an inverted Equilateral Triangle (or an upside down pyramid shape) is shaded surrounding the Vitruvian Man's left eye, whilst a more Circular shape exists shaded surrounding his right eye.

Based upon the preceding observational facts, the theory thereby considers that (through his creation of the Vitruvian Man) Leonardo da Vinci may've been evidently inferring that the *duo hemispheres of brain* are somehow connected to the *duo of polarities* of our shared cosmos (as previously discussed)—wherein Dark versus Light is one such approach for conceptualizing as much (further discussed in Chapter 7)—of such a *dual nature* that can also simultaneously exist within any conceptualized "thing" (of a premise also further detailed within Chapter7).

Such observational facts and consideration may lead one to assume that Leonardo knew (over 500 years ago) that the human brain had a *duo of hemispheres*—given the scientific work he physically performed on human anatomy—and by DaVinci drawing ONLY the Vitruvian Man's head tilting towards the right hemisphere (or halve) of the dissected circle that as much may be part of encoded hinting (or cues) related to a broader cryptic message (of such a proposed message further discussed throughout this book).

Resultant to such exposure (or revelation), it's thereby proposes that the Vitruvian Man schematic (in part) is an artistic commentary on *Sacred Geometry* identified NOT ONLY within the physical realm—as embodied within human anatomy, as previously determined by the Ancient Roman architect Marcus Vitruvius Pollio— BUT ALSO upon as much within the non-physical realm (specifically concerning *Mentalism*; term previously defined) whereby such *Sacred Geometric* patterns could identifiably exist within the shape, state, or condition of human psychology and behaviour.

In other words that by Leonardo, within the Vitruvian Man, recycling the determinations of Vitruvius—over 1,400 years beyond such ancient discovery—that Da Vinci was NOT ONLY paying homage to Vitruvius for such intelligent *Sacred Geometrical* analysis (hence the honoring name of the schematic) BUT ALSO, by Da Vinci using such an elaborate artistic format for reissuing (and showcasing) Vitruvius's physical realm determinations, that such a design could serve as an ingenious display to embed encoded messaging concerning *Sacred Geometrical* patterns that he may've conceptualized exists as per the less obvious non-physical realm (primarily relating to that of the psychological, or mental).

Any legitimate efforts to determine the reason for why Leonardo da Vinci may've deemed it necessary to curiously embed such proposed messaging within the

Vitruvian Man schematic perhaps would require an additional book of largely speculative nature.

This Vitruvian Man theory revolves around 4 main notions:

1. *Sacred Geometric* analysis can be employed towards identifying such non-physical patterns associated to psychology (or within *Mentalism*), and possibly also applicable within such analysis of resultant shapes, states, or conditions of any related behaviour chosen to be actuated into the physical realm
2. The reason such theorized messaging is embedded within the schematic's design is, in part, to issue timeless warning upon potentially dangerous elements considered existent (or perpetually looming) within the observance (or cerebral adoption) of a certain philosophical approach (or mental system) identified as constitutionally part of *Hermeticism*; whereby such a proposed warning would directly relate to why Da Vinci drew ONLY the Vitruvian Man's head tilting towards the right half (or hemisphere) of the schematic's circle once vertically dissected
3. Once necessary awareness has been established, *Dualism* becomes more obvious to observe within both the realms of the physical and non-physical
4. Leonardo da Vinci inevitably became to study certain *Sacred Geometric* approach and perspective

More full technical analysis of the Vitruvian Man schematic, as it pertains to the theory brought forth throughout this book, is found within the section titled "ADDITIONAL NOTE FOUR" (being the final section of this book).

CHAPTER 6

Hermeticism

The theory proposes that *Hermeticism*, *Sacred Geometry*, and *Dualism*, are 3 philosophical (or metaphysical) approaches of *disproportionate importance* (furthered below) for the purposes of certain practicing (or practitioner) members of so-called 'secretive societies'; in referring to how as much can be *specifically applied* within *Mentalism*.

NOTE: that the term *"specifically applied"* is considered referable to within a particular seeking and searching (and/or within a sort of science and study) of/for supra-concentrated forms of *Mentalism* wherein said 3 philosophical approaches can ultimately (disturbingly) be parlayed toward/within keen efforts to discover (or to conjure) potent mental techniques and psychological methodologies associated to *Mental Alchemy* (term defined within this chapter)

Such aforesaid *"disproportionate importance"* is meant to be considered within a context of how greatly important these 3 philosophical approaches are proposed to be for these relatively small groups of people, internally to/within such 'societies', compared to how relatively unimportant these 3 philosophical approaches consciously seem to be for disproportionately larger segments of citizenries (around the world) that socially exist external to such shrouded and esoterically veiled 'societies'.

For the purposes of this book, *Mental Alchemy* is defined as:

A comprehensive term for any sort of psychological, philosophical, or metaphysical science designed for/ to aid the study, development, and learning of better techniques, strategies, and methodologies for controlling one's own mind and potentially of that of others.

For the purposes of this book, Alchemy solely refers to:

Mental Alchemy.

NOTE: that the term Alchemy historically has also been used in reference to a sort of natural science concerned with the hopeful transformation of base metals (such as tin or lead) into those of greater value (such as silver or gold)

Typical elitist social (or societal) engineers are considered to have historically perceived great value and intelligence within *Mental Alchemical* studies and science. This is proposed as so given a suspicion that such elitists typically are psychologically fuelled by an excessive competitive interest, imbalanced drive, or obsessive compulsiveness to endlessly pursue the devising of better strategies and systems to assure that populations can increasingly be considered optimally controllable.

This touches on such typical elitist interest within the study of Mass Psychology wherein as much is proposed to inherently involve (consciously or otherwise) a concern for the mental (or electrochemical) conditioning (a.k.a. such *Mental Alchemy*) concerning masses of people.

It is proposed that *Ancient Hermeticism* (as with most major theisms or doctrines; consciously or otherwise, to varying degrees) directly embroils itself within *Mental Alchemy* (or such related psychological processes) by virtue of how such an all-encompassing theistic approach (or spiritual philosophy) is considered so very powerful (or effective) in shaping and sculpting an individual's electrochemical (or cerebral) development and/or as much of that of a group of people

NOTE: that such philosophical (thereby psychological) influences are proposed as particularly applicable toward the shaping and sculpting of how one inevitably perceives themselves within the contexts of a temporal, a universal, or an existential nature; whereby as much is proposed to directly influence the shape, state, or condition in which an individual's brain inevitably mentally (or electrochemically) forms and functions, and with regard to the manner as much relates to situational affect for how an individual may generally envision (or perceive) themselves within any given social hierarchy

Within the book *The Secret History of Hermes Trismegistus*, author Florian Ebeling (translated by David Lorton) essentially explains how *Hermeticism* is quite an all-encompassing term which touches on so many aspects of life (as do most major theisms). However, *Hermeticism* is a spiritual (or metaphysical) philosophy (or theistic approach) that readily incorporates the term "alchemy" (interpreted to mean *Mental Alchemy* for the purposes of this book) for which Ebeling basically states has often (historically) been referred to as "the Hermetic art" or "the Hermetic philosophy".[6]

Hermeticism is discussed more thoroughly throughout this book, but for now is put forth the contention that *Hermeticism* (within the concept—or "thing"—of Theism) offers *dual, polar,* or antithetical contrast to the theistic ideal of a more open and transparent form of Christianity whereby:

- both theisms propose the son of a god, whilst Hermes being the mythical son of Zeus (an idealized *power god*) whereas Jesus Christ a *prince of peace*
- a more common (or average) person may see *greater wisdom* within the principles and

---

[6] Florian Ebeling, *The Secrets of Hermes Trismegistus: Hermeticism from Ancient to Modern Times* (Ithaca and London: Cornell University Press, 2007), 103-108.

practices of a truly open ideal of Christianity— considered of whenever one's personal suffering is truly attempted to be understood (or embraced) within a spiritual intentionality of to energetically share (within whatever effort to help mitigate) any surmised physically catastrophic, emotionally devastating, or mentally crippling struggles another may be in the throes of—whereas, contrastingly, an elitist may see *greater intelligence* within the principles and practices of a more self-serving, veiled, or esoteric *Hermeticism*

NOTE: that *wisdom* and *intelligence* are antithetically conceptualized as per a paradoxical setting of opposite, opposing, or counterbalancing *forces of duality* within a context of *Mentalism* (as term defined in Chapter 1)

Thereby, summarily, within the concept (or "thing") of Theism, such *dual contrast* is proposed to exist along a spectrum measuring degrees of transparency (and/or a measure of the level of openness in communication concerning true intentionality of metaphysical mission) when comparing the greatly more esoteric *power theism* of *Hermeticism* against the ideal of a more truly open and populace form of Christianity.

Furthermore, the ideal of a *power theism* is considered to more broadly thrive and permeate within social ecosystems and climates wherever there exists excessive normalization of general measures of morality characterized (or defined) by whenever it is increasingly deemed 'holy' (or powerful) the more legal, or simply perceived, control one accrues over other things and stuff (including over any sort of property, other entities, or as much over the minds of other humans).

NOTE: that the term *"power theism"* is consideration to include both *Hermeticism* and Satanism as these 2 *power theisms* temporally centre themselves around the worship of core images (or idols) in the *power deities* of Zeus and Satan respectively

Practitioners (or observers) of such *power theisms* are proposed to perceive it normal (or necessary)—as per gonzo elitist logic—to form more 'secretive societies' given that such sorts of personalities tend to be psychologically characterized (in part) by:

- an excessive/imbalanced general distrust of their fellow humans
- an excessive/imbalanced fear of losing an idealized ('magical') psychological power (or mental ability) perceived to be personally aligned with, mastered, or held within themselves (or as much perceived to be in possession of, or in control of, over others)
- an excessive/imbalanced fear of public exposure to the truer nature of internally practiced philosophy, principles, or doctrine within such 'society'
- an excessive/imbalanced fear of losing procured, or accrued, physical possessions and/or such fear of losing control of any assumed seats-of-power held within any social hierarchy

Before temporarily pausing the discussion on *Hermeticism* (to be revisited within Chapter 8 of this book), this seems an appropriate spot to offer discussion upon some evident signs that *Hermeticism* has survived into our modern era, including:

- Hermes's Caduceus (considered a pagan symbol) is currently a major symbol (or insignia) for the institution and practice of modern medicine
- substantial modern populace suspicion that at the center of certain so-called 'secretive societies'— such as within both Freemasonry and Skull and Bones (a.k.a. The Brotherhood of Death)—found is the honouring of pagan deities (such as Thoth, Zeus, and Hermes Trismegistus) while, at the same time, a perplexingly large disproportionate number of positions (or roles) within Western society's most prominent institutions are filled by members of either Freemasonry, Skull and Bones, or from the Rhodes Scholarship program; as such positional-roles have been filled, in similar style, over the past 100 years at least

NOTE: that Cecil Rhodes—namesake and founding benefactor (upon his death) of the Rhodes Scholarship program—was most likely (while physically alive) of a power-soaked level and degree of Freemasonry

Incidentally many U.S. Founding Fathers were Freemasons, while other such Fathers were more of Rosicrucian association and philosophy—whilst

some members of such situational congress were of simultaneous association—ultimately Rosicrucianism concerns itself with *Hermeticism* and *Mental Alchemy* (term previously defined).
https://en.m.wikipedia.org/wiki/Rosicrucianism

Ironically while many modern-day Rhodes Scholars declare publicly that racism is of the most supremely abhorrent characteristics a human can possibly embody, indeed nary a Rhodes Scholar seems as impassioned about enacting such public condemnation upon Cecil Rhodes for clearly racist ideas expressed within his writings. The fact is that Cecil Rhodes had been recorded as stating, on behalf of the English (Anglo) race, "I contend that we are the first race in the world, and that the more of the world we inhabit the better it is for the human race."[7]

The following 4 historically significant occurrences transpired during the earlier years of the 20th century leading up to the beginning of the nightmarish WWI:

1. a first major Western modern-era governmental usage of the Hermetic Caduceus, as a symbol of medicine, was instituted by the U.S. Army Medical Corps in 1902[8]

---

[7] Cecil Rhodes (author) and William Thomas Stead (editor), *The Last Will and Testament of Cecil John Rhodes, with Elucidatory Notes, to which are Added Some Chapters Describing the Political and Religious Ideas of the Testator* (London: 1902), 58.
[8] Bernice Engle, *The Use of Mercury's Caduceus as a Medical Emblem* (CAMWS: The Classical Journal; December, 1929), 204-208.

2. the infamous U.S. Eugenics movement was essentially borne into the public sphere of consciousness, of a particular forceful promotion by at least 1906, that was given such momentum by certain eccentric elitists https://www.nicholls.edu/cheniere/2021/05/20/eugenics-in-the-united-states-the-forgotten-movement/

3. the Rhodes Scholarship was established, in 1903, following the death of Cecil Rhodes

4. *The Kybalion*—as aforementioned being the Hermetic handbook (of sorts)—was published in 1908

CHAPTER 7

Dualism (main discussion)

As pointed toward upon the end of Chapter 1, the *Dualism* (a.k.a. the *duality of force*; a.k.a. the *duo of polarities*; a.k.a. the *dual polarity*; a.k.a. the *dual nature*) existing within the following 12 "things" are here subjected to further analysis:

NOTE: that such further analysis is considered analogous with the aforecited Hermetic "principle of polarity"

1. ATOMIC MASS OF ELEMENTS: wherein Hydrogen (an element of the Lightest atomic mass, whilst simultaneously of the highest relative degree of instability), versus, Plutonium (an element of the Heaviest atomic mass, whilst also simultaneously of the highest relative degree of instability), represent the antithetical (or counterbalancing) ends of an elemental spectrum of measured mass (and/or a spectrum of the differing number of protons residing within the nucleus of each atom) that cumulatively comprise the Periodic Table of Elements; while each

element respectively ranges (along such spectrum) between this set of paradoxical parameters (or outer limits) innately constituted in accordance with the *dual nature* inherently existing within the same "thing"—the "thing", in this case, being the concept of ATOMIC MASS OF ELEMENTS; whereby such elements situationally exist while having diverged (by the number of such protons plus or minus) away from Iron; Iron being the most stable/balanced element of mass within a physical universe that sees each element (over time) intrinsically work to transmute itself toward becoming Iron

2. ELECTRICAL CHARGE: wherein Positive charge, versus, Negative charge, represent the antithetical (or counterbalancing) ends of a spectrum of measure ranging amidst the *dual nature* inherently existing within the same "thing"—the "thing", in this case, being the concept of ELECTRICAL CHARGE

3. WAVE FORM (be it a sine wave, wind wave, light wave, sound wave, or ocean wave): wherein the High peak of the natural oscillation of a wave form, versus, the Low peak of the natural oscillation of a wave form, represent the antithetical (or counterbalancing) ends of a spectrum of measurable points (of varying degrees) ranging along such a wave that cumulatively comprise the sum total of the form; while each said measurable point exists (within/along the

spectrum) ranging between this set of paradoxical parameters (or outer limits) innately constituted in accordance with the *dual nature* inherently existing within the same "thing"—the "thing", in this case, being the concept of WAVE FORM; whereby such measurable varying degrees (or such points along the wave) exist while having diverged (in either direction) away from a most neutral/balanced centrepoint-of-measure (in such case can be considered as the centered, neutral, or zeroed charge for a sine wave)

4. EMOTION/SENSATION: wherein Glee and Euphoric Mania, versus, Melancholy and Depressed Disillusionment, can represent the antithetical (or counterbalancing) ends of a spectrum of emotion ranging between this set of paradoxical parameters (or outer limits) innately constituted in accordance with the *dual nature* that inherently exists within the same "thing"— the "thing", in this case, being the concept of EMOTION/SENSATION; whereby such degrees of emotional variance exist while having diverged (in either direction) away from a most neutral/ balanced centrepoint-of-measure (in such case perhaps being within the neutral/balanced ideal of a Zen State of Mind)

5. TEMPERATURE: wherein extremely Hot, versus, extremely Cold, represent the antithetical (or counterbalancing) ends of a spectrum of temperature ranging between this set of

paradoxical parameters (or outer limits) innately constituted in accordance with the *dual nature* inherently existing within the same "thing"— the "thing", in this case, being the concept of TEMPERATURE; whereby such varying degrees of temperature exist while having diverged (in either direction) away from a most neutral/ balanced centrepoint-of-measure (in such case perhaps being within a neutral/balanced state of normal body temperature)

6. MAGNETIC EARTH: wherein the magnetic North Pole, versus, the magnetic South Pole, represent the antithetical (or counterbalancing) ends of a spectrum of measure ranging amidst the *dual nature* inherently existing within the same "thing"—the "thing", in this case, being the concept of MAGNETIC EARTH

7. MAMMILIAN GENDER: wherein Male, versus, Female, represent the antithetical (or counterbalancing) ends of a spectrum of measure ranging amidst the *dual nature* inherently existing within the same "thing"—the "thing", in this case, being the concept of MAMMILIAN GENDER

8. SOCIABILITY OF PERSONALITY: wherein extremely Introverted, versus, extremely Extroverted, represent the antithetical (or counterbalancing) ends of a spectrum of such sociability ranging between this set of paradoxical parameters (or outer limits) innately constituted in accordance with the *dual nature* inherently

existing within the same "thing"—the "thing", in this case, being the concept of SOCIABILITY OF PERSONALITY; whereby such degrees of variance exist while having diverged (in either direction) away from a most neutral/balanced centrepoint-of-measure (in such case perhaps being of what some may consider a normal personality)

9. WESTERN POLITIC: wherein extreme Left, versus, extreme Right, represent the antithetical (or counterbalancing) ends of a spectrum of such politic ranging between this set of paradoxical parameters (or outer limits) innately constituted in accordance with the *dual nature* inherently existing within the same "thing"—the "thing", in this case, being the concept of WESTERN POLITIC; whereby such degrees of political variance are conceptualized to exist while having diverged (in either direction) away from a most neutral/balanced centrepoint-of-measure (in such case perhaps being of what some would call a political centrist)

Whereas within 1930's Germany, as well within other nations during those years, the great political debate was between *extreme Left (Communism)* versus *extreme Right (Fascism)* where certain party leaders (within this type of *extreme polarity-of-politic*) tend to be of such unbalanced, polarized, and polarizing mindsets that such associated citizenries become increasingly likely to get consumed and taken by the same polarized (and polarizing) mental infection (or psychological illness) given that most such citizens tend to search for intellectual and social guidance by looking toward their selected party leaders and media personalities—while such leading charismatic and inflammatory personalities can often be the incendiary sources of what may eventually spread epidemically (in such instances), from human-host to human-host, of a polarized/polarizing sort of mental (or emotional) mania—whereby such a psychological (or mental) virus is proposed as able to become electrochemically agitated (or stimulated) to spread so impulsively, of such speed and effectiveness, that as much could possibly make a standard coronavirus figuratively blush given inferior related abilities.

10. *ARCHETYPE GEOMETRIC SHAPES* (of geometric shape wherein its perimeter is comprised of only equal length straightedged sides, or line segments): whereby the Equilateral Triangle (Least geometrically dynamic, of the Least possible amount of equal length straightedged line segments for to comprise the perimeter of an *archetype geometric shape*), versus, the Circle (Most geometrically dynamic, whereas the Circle can be conceptualized as either having ZERO or an INFINITE number of such line segments comprising its circumference, or perimeter), represent the antithetical (or counterbalancing) ends of a spectrum of geometric dynamism

ranging between this set of paradoxical parameters (or outer limits) innately constituted in accordance with the *dual nature* inherently existing within the same "thing"— the "thing", in this case, being the concept of *ARCHETYPE GEOMETRIC SHAPES*; whereby such varying degrees of geometric dynamism are conceptualized to exist while having diverged (in either direction) away from a most neutral/balanced centrepoint-of-measure

11. THEISM: a Peace-advising god, versus, a War-advising god, is proposed to represent the antithetical (or counterbalancing) ends of a spectrum of theistic approach ranging between this set of paradoxical parameters (or outer limits) innately constituted in accordance with the *dual nature* inherently existing within the same "thing"—the "thing", in this case, being the concept of THEISM; whereby such degrees of variance within theistic approach are conceptualized to exist while having diverged (in either direction) away from a most neutral/balanced centrepoint-of-measure [in such case, considerable perhaps as being any sort of substantial departure away from the ideal of a Buddhist Middle Way mentality of nothingness, whereas when one exists to compete excessively within worldly systems then the individual is considered more likely to experience (consciously or otherwise) an intensified concurrent beckoning

from both *metaphysical directionalities* (a.k.a.
from such cosmic *duality of force*) thereby seeming
to promise such actors, upon the continuum of
worldly stages, a dramatic range (or spectrum) of
perpetually unfolding paradoxical experiences—
across space and time—amidst the intrinsically
dual theatre of temporal existence]

Such a proposed premise of *dual* (or paradoxical)
"metaphysical directionality" existing within the concept
(or "thing") of THEISM thereupon positions the lifepaths
eventually chosen and pursued by people such as Abraham,
Moses, Mother Theresa, Gautama Buddha, Confucius,
Jesus Christ, Mahatma Gandhi, and Martin Luther King
(of people where seeking such related guidance from an
envisioned Peace-advising god seemed more of preeminent
importance), set in POLAR CONTRAST against the
lifepaths eventually chosen and pursued by people such
as Alexander the Great, Caesar Augustus, Mohammed,
Justinian I, Genghis Khan, Vlad the Impaler, Suleiman the
Magnificent, Ivan the Terrible, and Napoleon (of people
where seeking such related guidance from an envisioned
War-advising god seemed more of preeminent importance).

The theory, as brought forth throughout this book,
offers that such *dual forces* (so innately paradoxical)
at play within human nature disallows any individual
to presume, nor claim, to be of "perfect" philosophical
ideals (nor metaphysical practice) while physically alive.
However, the aforesaid comparatively more Peace-
advised (or advising) people are proposed to have

ultimately committed toward paths more associated with enlightened (or enlightening) philosophical (or metaphysical) creed (certainly while considering their observed and recorded conduct during the more final chapters of their respective life-stories) despite any sort of Dark ideations perhaps more once embodied before (or even possibly actuated into the physical world) by such proposed people.

It's assumed that the idea of "perfection" cannot exist in relation to protracted measures of anything associated to human nature. The contention is that its more likely that some thing, or some theory, would be idealistically assumed to be of "perfection" within (or due to) absolutist philosophical realms, arenas, or approaches associated to (or involving) mathematical calculation and theory.

Concerning those comparatively more War-advised (or advising) aforesaid people—of people assumed more likely to deem it righteous (or necessary) to embrace theistic (or philosophical) creed wherein more positive aspects of War are perceived than negative—such people are considered to have possibly led otherwise Peace-seeking cultures (or such societies) toward War upon any sort of successful rationalizations (to be deemed, or perceived, of righteous action to manifest into the physical world) for the enactment of lethal decrees-for-action.

Furthermore the proposal is that War set into action, beyond any such action reasonably set in self-defence, may eventually become Darkly rationalized as 'righteous' (in a metaphysically distorted sense) wherein any sort of designs, devises, or desires for War can relativity swiftly (as history has proven) become parlayed into the War of empire-building; whilst considering that such War could've originally been fuelled by/within some sort of more avenging premise searching for a sense of "settling a score" perhaps for a perceived wrong done upon an individual, group, or nation.

Within robust efforts to consider for why such an imbalanced/ excessively Dark psychological aforesaid 'righteousness' is even capable of developing in the first place, it's proposed more likely to develop within an entity—being that of an individual, institution, or nation—once such related behavioural patterns have been successfully rationalized increasingly for enactment into the physical world—thereby proposed as becoming increasingly electrochemically normalized within a brain and body—then such behaviour is more likely to become of a patterned mental addiction (assuming any sort of positive feedback was perceived and/ or experienced during such course).

NOTE: that wherewith the preceding understanding is applied toward consideration for such a growing military empire, associated leading elitist-mindsets may more 'normally' (in a distorted sense) necessarily perceive MORE great Darkness within other nations, cultures, and peoples, THAN any possibly *perceived great Darkness to have been ignorantly allowed to develop within themselves, and within such an associated expanding military empire*

Such said "possibly *perceived great Darkness to have been ignorantly allowed to develop within themselves, and within such an associated expanding military empire*" was stated as so granted the mental ease, and situational delight, that can exist in ignoring that which is proposed to potentially grow unconsciously (or unattended to psychologically) within the mysterious Dark depths of human psyche—of such Darkness proposed able to curiously develop within an individual, or to possibly grow cumulatively (consciously or otherwise) within the conceptualized premise of a nation's mass (or collective) psyche—while lacking adequate counterbalancing degrees of focused psychological attention, revealment, or exposure.

This may be a point in the report where some Jungian analysis is necessary (or apropos) within any sort of qualified attempt to understand how, or for why, such mysterious psychological developments can (or are able to) grow within any given human.
https://www.azquotes.com/author/7659-Carl_Jung/tag/darkness

12. METAPHYSICAL (or SPIRITUAL) PHILOSOPHY; wherein 7 differing such approaches (as detailed below) contain such various ways for to conceptualize the *dual nature* existing within the same "thing"—the "thing", in this case, being the concept of METAPHYSICAL (or SPIRITUAL) PHILOSOPHY:

a. Light versus Dark [of a Native North American approach for conceptualizing the *dual polarity* identified as per the cosmos (or mental universe)]

b. Good versus Evil [of an Abrahamic approach for conceptualizing the *dual polarity* identified as per the cosmos (or mental universe)]

c. Yin versus Yang [of an Ancient Chinese approach for conceptualizing the *dual polarity* identified as per the cosmos (or mental universe)]

d. Eternalism versus Annihilationism [of a Buddhist—Middle Way—approach for conceptualizing the *dual polarity* identified as per the cosmos (or mental universe)]

e. Circle versus Equilateral Triangle [of a proposed *Sacred Geometric* approach for conceptualizing the *dual polarity* identified as per the cosmos (or mental universe); of such an approach considered directly linked to the *dually shaded* shapes respectively surrounding the Right and Left eyes of Vitruvian Man]

Within the context of applying a sort of *Sacred Geometric* approach within an analysis of social hierarchy, the theory proposes that a premised *Excessively Triangulated Social Hierarchy*—tending to be characterized by extremely high degrees of stringent psychological conditioning—can be of such heavy-handed, impressing, and relentless social pressure (or tenor) that a tyrannically oppressing and coercive air (or social climate) may be produced (possibly of a seeming omnipresence) wherein its members, or potential members, could deem is absolutely necessary to develop personally-conforming adaptive (or coping) strategies possibly of a metaphysically (or spiritually) blinding affect.

NOTE: that the development of such "personally-conforming adaptive (or coping) strategies" is considered of a higher likelihood to occur if such social circumstances present themselves where such a psychological technique (or methodology) could increasingly seem (consciously or otherwise) as a reasonable (or potentially helpful) mental strategy, for adoption, while perhaps desperately trying to figure out effective ways and means to maintain one's sanity while operating, existing, or functioning within such a terrorizing social hierarchy

Within such a proposed psychological scenario, an individual may deem it intelligent to succumb to a certain polarizing call for the intellectual adherence to (or for the cerebral capitulation toward) such a siren call (if you will) for the Annihilation (in an extreme Buddhist sense) of whatever previous version of themselves (of which they may've envisioned before existed)—in order to adequately fulfill the duties (depending on what is demanded of them) involved with whatever position to be assumed while operating, existing, or functioning within such an *Excessively Triangulated Social Hierarchy*—that the results, upon such "previous version of themselves", may involve such a destructive (or at least materially compromising) effect that as much may seem to have been *Triangulated upon* (as within a seek-and-destroy, in order to rebuild, militant effect); whereas, within a geometrically contrasting sense, the Circle (as per the continuation of such proposed *Sacred Geometric* approach for analysis) has many times been associated to the shape of a halo, one's spiritual aura, or the metaphysical (or spiritual) premise of Eternalism (as within an aforesaid Buddhist extreme sense).

NOTE: that such severely unbalanced controlling-systems (or such *Excessively Triangulated Social Hierarchy*) could be confused for systems designed to encourage and foster the normalization of a seeming hell on earth

The theory contends that if such social ecosystems exist and function of greater *Sacred Geometric balance* within approach and form—thereby proposed as systems that are somehow capable of greater dynamics, faculty, and capacity for the better true consideration of (or the more humane attendance toward) the associated needs (or callings) from both the realms of the physical and non-physical—then such a resultant system (in such state, form, or condition) is considered more likely to indefinitely sustain itself into the future given the observational fact that every excessively triangulated hierarchical empire (or such type system-of-control) which formed before, over the course of recorded history, inevitably collapsed; except for such existing systems that have not collapsed (while as much may be of a possible inevitability).

f. Positive versus Negative [of a New Age approach for conceptualizing the *dual polarity* identified within the cosmos (or mental universe)]

g. Above versus Below [of an Ancient Greco-Roman Hermetic approach for conceptualizing the *dual polarity* identified within the cosmos (or mental universe)]

CHAPTER 8

Hermeticism (within further discussion)

The doctrine of *Hermeticism* provides for the constructs of both *morality* and *Dualism* (Hermetically of the aforecited "principle of polarity") of which discussion within the following paragraphs works to simultaneously incorporate.

As per Hermetical doctrine, ABOVE—defined as THE ONE (or the deity Creator)—is understood as the ONLY THING that a Hermeticist can ever truly consider as GOOD within the universe, which apparently is of a Hermetic principle (or rationale) designed to reconcile the abundance of *Darkness* perceived (or estimated) to exist within 3rd dimensional physical existence and reality.

NOTE: that as per such analysis and subject matter, the term *"Darkness"* is proposed to include an identified excess of rationalized malicious acts perpetrated by humans for self-serving purposes, devises, or perceived personal gain; wherein such malicious acts are proposed to include an identified worldly excess of (or such accumulation of) rape, murder, war, psychology manipulation and attack, and all such maliciousness enacted relating to temptations for, and of, the flesh

BELOW, on the other hand (as per the doctrine), is understood to be essentially everything that exists which is not Hermetically defined as (nor considered to be) ABOVE—a.k.a. everything that is not defined as (nor considered to be) THE ONE Creator deity god; thereby logically (as per such Hermetical creed) conceptualizing all humans (and/or all aspects of human nature) as being philosophically *dually categorized* as BELOW.

NOTE: that by extrapolating upon such Hermetic logic, it's deduced that *Hermeticism* holds that humans cannot truly ever be considered GOOD, nor should humans ever reasonably be expected to be GOOD given accordance to such Hermetic principles providing that the ONLY GOOD in the universe is the deity Creator (THE ONE); thereby possibly offering a theistic philosophy designed (consciously or otherwise) to train, condition, or facilitate the development of mental, psychological, or cerebral patterns within a brain whereby the electrochemical relationship (or connection) between a human's body and its conscience may somehow become associatively bypassed as a result

Within efforts to understand how the idea of *morality* is approached within Hermetical creed, it's proposed that as much is designed to train, support, and encourage such practicing (or such seeking) Hermeticists to accept the notion that ONLY THE FAÇADE of acting in Good (within an Abrahamic extreme sense) ways and means is possible to conceptualize and enact into the physical world. This can be inferred to mean that an individual would only attempt to act Good if it was deemed necessary, possibly as per sorts of devised strategies designed to increase one's personal control over physical possessions, or to increase one's perceived psychological influence, sway, or control over another.

Moreover, such Hermetic logic seems to place no rational (nor reasonable) value in truly seeking to develop Goodness (within Abrahamic parlance) within one's self given Hermetical creed holding that the Creator (THE ONE; Hermetically ABOVE) is the ONLY GOOD that truly exists within the universe.

Hermeticism is considered able to be viewed in various ways including as a theistic philosophy, or as a *power theism*.

Perhaps such a *"power theism"* perspective (upon how to view *Hermeticism*) is most fitting as it seems an inhumanely competitive (or psychologically unbalancing) metaphysical approach for how to perceive the nature of the universe, and for one's place within it.

NOTE: that such associative mythology (or storylines) is founded within legend and lore where fathers grow extremely wary (or suspicious) that their sons will inevitably plan (as only a matter of time) to overthrow their father's perceived position-of-power atop a family hierarchy, where a father (as a result) tragically seeks to devour his children (as babies) upon birth, and where previously swallowed (or devoured) sons nonsensically do somehow eventually launch such once feared hostile bids to seize their father's positions atop such insanely competitive family hierarchies

Such depicted scenarios are proposed as more likely to manifest and unfold within extremely competitive social environments, groups, or families, while such said hierarchical developments did indeed take place amid the mythical power-covetous family story found at the center of Ancient Greek Paganism.

It is proposed that the origins of such legendary hierarchical (or family) tales are highly likely to have developed (or generated) from such sorts of tragic scenarios playing out, in the flesh, within the various elitist royal houses and imperial courts throughout time, all around the world, but particularly as how this specific legend grew through Ancient Greece and/or through such culturally (historically) related Mediterranean *power houses*; Hermes being a mythical Greek deity.

Associated to (or at the center of) such Ancient Greek Pagan mythology is indeed a power-covetous family story that begins primordially upon the creation of the universe. Such legend tells of titanic tales that play out within a terribly contentious family hierarchy that saw the patriarch, Cronus, siring Zeus; Zeus inevitably siring his son Hermes.

Such lore is full of calamitous power struggle that apparently provided the theistic, spiritual, or metaphysical foundation upon which the philosophical backbone of *Hermeticism* could be established to grow and develop.

Incidentally, these sorts of elitist-mindsets (as archetypally characterized by such mythological figures; of psychological arenas where the ends usually justify the means) are theorized to offer a psychological foundation, or a genesis of mentality, for the fostering of monopolistic desires to achieve ultimate control over all current (and potential) competition; whereby a possibly perceived need to Annihilate (in the Buddhist extreme sense) all such competition may eventually internally develop—proposed to be of extreme degrees of anti-social monopolistic obsessive desire.

The theory considers that experiencing too much time existing (or competing) within such excessively vicious, and arguably inhumane, social ecosystems can offer *a certain sort of cerebral encouragement* (discussed below) for an individual to increasingly perceive such incessant psychological warfare (and such related mind-games) as an alluring and just method for social conduct.

NOTE: that such "*a certain sort of cerebral encouragement*" is proposed to exist ever-present within such social ecosystems (and social climates) wherein certain Dark psychological elements can hang (or waft) intrinsically dormant awaiting, predatorily, for anyone to foolishly get hooked by such pulling, ensnaring, or seducing social elements upon figurative battlefields of psychological warfare wherein overly-impressionable brains can swiftly get made

Given the proposal that most elitist social settings naturally encourage (consciously or otherwise) a normalization of such polarized (and/or polarizing) mindsets, it's thereby considered generally not unusual (dependant upon circumstance) for the resultantly most extreme polarized mindsets to perceive the destruction of any current, or potential future, competition as reasonable means for how to consider (or for how to conceptualize) the fact that such competition even exist at all.

As a result, it is proposed that such most extremely conditioned (or polarized) personalities invariably become to prefer (to much higher relative degrees) some sort of monopolistic form of competition in comparison to more open, less corrupted, forms of competition; of such a polarized preference that's considered substantially contrastable to the degree of preference, for a fairer form of competition, assumed to be held by a more common (or regular) type of personality.

In the ancient world, as the elitist Roman rulers adopted such fellow elitist Greco theistic philosophy (and/

or cultural mythology): Cronus became Saturn, Zeus became Jupiter, and Hermes became Mercury.

In typical gonzo elitist fashion, such Ancient Greco myth is renown for Cronus growing so extremely paranoid and consumed by a vision, passed along by an oracle—which foretold that Conus's children would inevitably grow up to launch hostile challenge for his seat-of-power, just as Cronus had similarly before launched upon his father (Uranus)—that Cronus tragically saw it intelligent to swallow his children upon their birth.

NOTE: that such monstrous scenarios—wherein a baby boy is devoured (or swallowed) by his father (as per insanely sinister stratagem to preserve his own power)— may either wickedly echo, or ominously ring, of twisted Satanic scenes in where the only thing that truly matters is to pursue the full appeasement of one's own unchecked (or unbalanced) Dark impulses to serve thyself

To reiterate, the Ancient Greco *power deity*, Cronus, eventually became Satan...er...ah...Saturn within Ancient Roman culture.

NOTE: that perhaps here it's relevant (or applicable) to recall that Jesus was once referred to as Yeshua—of his original Aramaic name—whereby many historical names have changed, over time, as the various linguistic translations took place

Relatedly, many photos are easily accessible on the internet that show clear evidentiary congruence between Satanical and Hermetical imagery; with particular reference to a large standing statute (within America) of the Satanic Baphomet—built tall and wide with children gazing up toward this goat-headed creature—created and constructed, blended together, with the double-snake helix formation (that's associated to the Hermetic Caduceus) arising from its groin area.

NOTE: that Hermes's son (or Cronus's great grandson) is Pan; being a mythical deity that is legendarily (disturbingly) of similar appearance to the goat-headed Satanic Baphomet creature
https://en.m.wikipedia.org/wiki/Pan_(god)

Given such aforesaid narratives, perhaps it is relevant here to question from where did the name *Satan* originally derive?

Popular internet etymology of the name *Satan* puts forth the contention that its linguistic usage dates back at least 500 years prior to the birth of Jesus Christ, whereby *Satan* is essentially proposed as a metaphysical force associated with the polarity of Darkness that perpetually stands running contrary to (or continually devising against) the human way that corresponds with a spiritual mission (of sorts) for to be pushed dimensionally higher—as per such connected calling from within toward without—whilst to ultimately be marginally more (at least by the slightest majority amount more) mentally aligned with the counterbalancing polarity bound to Enlightenment.

NOTE: that the Ancient Greeks were a ravishing naval (military) powerhouse within (and around) a Mediterranean Sea shared by those referenced cultures said to have been of such original cautionary usage of the term *Satan*; while, perhaps unconnectedly, many elitist-minded Ancient Greeks honoured a 'titanic' *power god* (Cronus) of which fellow elitist-minded Romans would later go on to rename Saturn and thusly praise accordingly

Incidentally (while of possibly unrelated information) there exists a circulating gaseous pattern, of hexagon shape, that is titanically-sized residing on one of Saturn's planetary poles—of such colossal size that the diameter of the gaseous pattern is wider than that of planet Earth— while a hexagon has 6 equal length straightedged sides (or line segments), 6 points (tips to the shape), and 6 interior angles.
https://en.m.wikipedia.org/wiki/Saturn%27s_hexagon

Such a narrative potentially dispels the historically cryptic number 666 as more of an obvious mathematical (or geometric) association; whereas, along the way, an artifice of myth and fear may've been purposefully stoked (by uber elitist-mindsets) as to gin up excessive amounts of apprehension, to surround such Dark ideations and imagery, while perversely envisioning as much being part of some sort of deviant psychological process imagined as necessary for the foundation (or creation) of what can pathologically be considered a useful, effective, or powerful psychic-tool (of sorts) that could somehow be parlayed within a typical elitist's beloved pastime in the brainstorming about how to increasingly manipulate the minds of others—whereby as much is all proposed as being somehow associated to elaborate mental-games possibly linked to a mysterious source of convoluted pleasure for a relatively small number of people (or groups) with heavy historical interest in social-engineering the minds of others.

The hexagram (or the so-called 6-pointed star; a.k.a. the Star of David) has 6 points, 6 smaller-sized equilateral triangles (intrinsically present within its patterned shape), and 6 missing curved line segments (of which would be necessary to superimpose, in a circumscribing fashion, so as to connect said 6 points together); of such circumscription necessary to create a superimposed circumference to surround (circularly) the hexagram in order to form the shape of a so-called *false circle* (or *false circle of light*) whereas the ideal of True Enlightenment—of the *true circle of light* (symbolically of a path related to True Enlightenment)—is more classically (or culturally, historically) associated to the more circular geometric shape of a halo, or that of a human's aura. https://en.m.wikipedia.org/wiki/Hexagram

NOTE: that the geometric shape of the hexagon naturally forms at the centre of the hexagram thereby creating a sort of geometric chicken and egg scenario (if one will)

The preceding narrative is offered within a Dr. Martin Luther King ideal (whilst considered to be of such associated reasoning) as per an allied model where it's essentially always considered better to have GAINED (one way or another) through communicating on certain knowledge rather than to allow any perhaps latent wisdom be possibly LOST resultant to a more fearful ignorance to willfully obstruct such potentially enlightening communicative-flows, all along hopeful spiritual (or metaphysical) paths wherein Dr. Martin Luther King's depth of wisdom could even more resonate among the masses.
https://www.goodreads.com/quotes/10800-people-fail-to-get-along-because-they-fear-each-other

The following question is here proposed as relevant to the subject matter at hand:

If Cronus (or Saturn) exists within the ideal of an original *power god* (and/or as a legendary primordial Titan of the Universe), then does there exist fundamental difference between the premise of Satan (biblically depicted as a worldly *power deity*) and that of Saturn (or Cronus) within efforts to define temporal (or worldly) *power deities*?

NOTE: that if such a question is indeed contemplated, perhaps it is necessary to keep in mind that within such Ancient Pagan lore...Cronus (or Saturn) was willing to devour his own children (upon their birth) as per devises to personally assure the preservation of his position of power; of a decision made, and action taken, while seemingly suffering from some sort of paranoid delusion upon mythically learning of a treacherous vision purveyed by an oracle whilst, incidentally, such obsessively neurotic behavioural traits of pathology—including the sufferance of excessively paranoid sensations—have classically been psychologically identified as common within many an exceedingly tyrannical personality type

Disturbingly, the preceding narrative can highlight the sort of high significance any sort of priest-class (or oracle) can have (or possess) within such sorts of related developments, especially if supremely elitist (or predatory) choices are selected whereby an employment (or deployment) of particularly serpentine strategy is launched into action designed to manipulate (or to capitalize upon; possibly for self-serving rationales) certain obvious defining psychological eccentricities (and/or evident mental imbalance) that tend to (or have tended to) exist within such excessively tyrannical and paranoid personality types associated to the various kings and emperors of history...which surely wouldn't be of a devilish sort of machination existing beyond the mental wherewithal of certain so-called 'holy men' of history.

Besides, within such specified legend concerning idealized (mythological) power-rings and the associative wrangling, Zeus and his two brothers (Poseidon and Hades) did inevitably somehow (after being swallowed as babies) overthrow their father's (Cronus's) seat-of-power

just as Cronus did of his father (Uranus) before, as per the lore.
https://en.m.wikipedia.org/wiki/Cronus

NOTE: that such legendary contradiction and/or such impossible simultaneous occurrence (as so expressed within Ancient Greek Pagan stories) can possibly serve to indicate significant metaphysical (or spiritual) confusion, whilst as much is proposed connectable to a particular psychological imbalance considered associated to whenever an individual excessively romanticizes (or excessively endears themselves toward) such ancient imagery and stories (of which correspond to a general universal perspective held within Ancient Greek Paganism; as relayed through *Hermeticism*)—whereby such psychological developments are proposed to go hand-in-hand with pathological behaviour proposed to current (or transmute) downstream from particular personality disorder of such Hermetic induction, mental conditioning, or electrochemical training (wherein such a human host could be argued as suffering from mental illness)

It is estimated that many of these Ancient Pagan (Hermetical) stories concern the plight of individuals, vying for high seats-of-power within viciously competitive social ecosystems, who personally fell prey to lopsided mental impulses (or compulsion) to attain, and hoard (if deemed appropriate and necessary) extreme measures of power and control, thereby to serve as dangerous figures (or idols) of history to excessively romanticize or endear one's self toward.

Such tragic legendary tales seem terribly so much about deity figures (of human image) internally succumbing to (or psychologically capitulating to) excessive, imbalanced, or unchecked mental impulses associated to neurosis, paranoia, and fear of physical loss. So much about plotting and scheming to increase an individual's personal position within metaphysically (or spiritually) warped institution and hierarchy.

The theory contends that the doctrine of *Hermeticism* can give (consciously or otherwise) practitioners a certain twisted (manipulated) perspective on *Dualism* wherein this particular theistic philosophy can offer a knowledgeable Hermeticist specified *rationales of reason* (discussed below) in support of the belief that a so-called 'Intelligent Design' exists universally, perpetually standing by, ready to spell out the logic for any given individual's choice to mentally, cerebrally, or electrochemically absolve one's self from an internal connection to the polarity of Good (in the Abrahamic extreme sense); in such a case, the perception may be considered always arguably in accordance with the Hermetical will of THE ONE.

Such said *"rationales of reason"* are proposed as supportable by Hermetical doctrine given as much prescribes that only THE ONE (The Creator; Hermetically ABOVE) can ever truly be considered

GOOD, which is interpreted as creed that can also serve to guide, foster, or encourage the assistance of the creation of potentially (or at least proposed to be) dangerously optimized psychological settings (or such mental mindsets) where theorized processes of *Mental Alchemy* (as term defined in Chapter 6) can occur and ensue wherein resultantly Hermetically conditioned brains are considered to have become electrochemically isolated away from the metaphysical polarity known as Good (within Abrahamic parlance); at least increasingly as much by way of such related cerebral (or cognitive) processes.

Furthermore, such an electrochemically isolating (mental) effect is theorized to manifest to correlatingly higher degrees commensurate to the degrees of time and effort that such doctrine is personally sought to be practiced, thereby instilled.

As much is stated as so given that Hermetical doctrine teaches that humans cannot reasonably be expected to be GOOD whilst The Creator God is Hermetically held as the ONLY thing within the universe truly capable of being GOOD; in other words, thereby possibly conditioning such a Hermetically isolated (or trained) brain to essentially (in its most extreme form) become ONLY able to electrochemically access the metaphysical polarity known as Evil (within Abrahamic parlance).

The theory contends that once such a Hermetically conditioned brain has been trained to disconnect (or disengage) its internal electrochemical connection to the counterbalancing metaphysical polarity of Good (within Abrahamic parlance), then such a brain is considered to have become *dangerously divided* from the electrochemical influence and affect associated with a human conscience.

Such said "*dangerously divided*" brain refers to a sort of potential sense in how such a Hermetically conditioned (or trained) brain would simultaneously be equipped with such *dual* knowledge and understanding (as per Hermetic teachings) whilst, in the most extreme cases, proposed to have become of a potentially dangerous embodied *dichotomy* of metaphysical imbalance.

NOTE: that the proposed result of such said "*dichotomy*" (in such a case being considered of an extreme degree of electrochemical isolation, separation, or division) can be where such an individual becomes mentally designed psychologically prime to optimally (dangerously) manipulate such *dual forces*, of which are more ordinarily (or naturally) existent (or at play) within others —others whom a trained Hermeticist may eventually develop desire to materially manipulate in order to establish mental dominion upon—all the while the Hermeticist is proposed to personally prefer (consciously or otherwise) a more *nondual* (or *isolated*) mental patterned shape, state, or condition electrochemically, given that ALL is considered fair play within Hermetic lore and legend (or within such psychological arenas) where a father may fearfully swallow (or devour) a son within desperate measures to preserve his own power

According to the theory brought forth throughout this book, such a seriously (or 'greatly'; as in Alexander the 'great' state-sponsored Mass Murderer) conditioned Hermetical mindset (or such an excessively trained elitist personality) is proposed (or presumed) to have so resolutely fallen prey to a particular internal impulse-based (or mental polar) encouragement to develop such an extreme preference—perhaps considered of a high degree of mental addiction—to physical existence and experience without the electrochemical burden (or such related electrochemical affects upon the body) associated to a human conscience.

As much is proposed of a psychological (or mental) shape, state, or condition—as much being fashioned of *nondual* zeal—that's been deduced as held (as well) in high esteem as per (or within) the apparent fellow elitist philosophy of Neoplatonism—wherein much intellectual overlap evidentially exists between *Hermeticism* and Neoplatonism whereby such current, or prospective, elitist members and initiates (to either philosophical type quest) are considered to prefer (or to seek, consciously or otherwise) a *nondualistic* alignment as per their own internally developed electrochemical patterns; while both such type quests are proposed as ultimately of excessively Dark metaphysical impulse and drive (as the next chapter will attempt to further detail, explore, and reveal).

CHAPTER 9

Neoplatonism

The following quote was selected from within a Wikipedia article titled *Neoplatonism*: https://en.m.wikipedia.org/wiki/Neoplatonism

> Neoplatonism is a strand of Platonic philosophy that emerged in the 3rd century AD against the background of Hellenistic philosophy and religion.[9] The term does not encapsulate a set of ideas as much as it encapsulates a chain of thinkers which began with Ammonius Saccas and his student Plotinus (c. 204/5 – 271 AD), which stretches to the 6th century AD.[10] Even though neoplatonism primarily circumscribes the thinkers who are now labeled neoplatonists

[9] Edward Moore (n.d.), *Neoplatonism* (Internet Encyclopedia of Philosophy, Retrieved 2 May 2019).

[10] Lucas Siorvanes, *"Plotinus and Neoplatonism: The Creation of a New Synthesis"*. In Paul Turquand Keyser and John Scarborough (eds.) *The Oxford Handbook of Science and Medicine in the Classical World* (New York: Oxford University Press), 847-868.

and not their ideas, there are some ideas that are common to neoplatonic systems; for example, the monistic idea that all of reality can be derived from a single principle, "the One"[11]

...Neoplatonism had an enduring influence on the subsequent history of philosophy. In the Middle Ages, neoplatonic ideas were studied and discussed by Christian, Jewish, and Muslim by thinkers. In the Islamic cultural sphere, neoplatonic texts were available in Arabic and Persian translations[12]...

...Neoplatonism also had a strong influence on the perennial philosophers of the Italian Renaissance thinkers Marsilio Ficino and Pico della Mirandola, and continues through nineteenth-century Universalism and modern-day spirituality and nondualism. Neoplatonism underpins

---

[11] Jens Halfwassen, *"The Metaphysics of the One"*. In Svetla Slaveva-Griffin and Pauliina Remes (eds.) *The Routledge Handbook of Neoplatonism*. Routledge Handbooks in Philosophy (Abingdon, Oxfordshire and New York: Routledge, 2014), 182-199.
[12] Howard Kreisel, *"Moses Maimonides"*. In Daniel Frank and Oliver Lehman (eds.) *History of Jewish Philosophy*. Routledge history of world philosophies (London and New York: Routledge, 1997), 245-280.

the mystical traditions in all three of the major Abrahamic religions.[13]

The following 6 commentaries address selected terms and names found discussed within the preceding quotation while working to connect as much to the theory proposed throughout this book. Such terms and names are itemized within the short list below in the order they will be discussed:

1. Plato, and his philosophical mentor Socrates
2. Nondualism
3. Plotinus
4. the One
5. Marsilio Ficino
6. Giovanni Pico della Mirandola

1. For the elitist Ancient Athenian state-controllers, Plato is proposed to have ultimately become more of an appeasing pinup-boy (in so many words) than became of Socrates (ironically being Plato's mentor); Socrates was more the populous favourite, whereas Plato had philosophized that slavery was a necessary part of society; where Socrates's state-administered 'reward' (or punishment) was the death sentence for his spending so much time walking the streets of Athens engaging with any particular human(s) he may've encountered

---

[13] Karen Armstrong, *A History of God*.

within apparent efforts to empower such people with his infusing ability to cognitively reason whilst Socrates simultaneously had (as the story goes) publicly warned on the potential folly of holding excessive amounts of faith in anything, or anyone, beyond such individual's ability to cognitively reason—which was said to include Socrates advising to not put excessive faith in any sort of Athenian state-controller, which may have sealed his fate—whereas Plato wrote *The Republic* (full of Socratic dialogues, not Platonic dialogues) about 15 years beyond Socrates's death thereby creating suspicion that such a generation-of-time was perhaps deemed strategically necessary to pass, before issuing Plato's *The Republic*, so as a hearty populous memory of Socrates could've had a better chance of being materially bent toward the controlling-will of a more state-backed elitist Platonic philosophy; incidentally Socrates was known to have not kept (nor created) physical record concerning his philosophical approaches thusly then-offering Plato circumstantial opportunity to potentially edit Socrates's teachings more in tune with how Plato's proposed governmental allies may've deemed it more suitable and advantageous for such Athenian state-interests.

2. *Nondualism* is assessed as a philosophical (or metaphysical) approach stemming as a natural such contrarian to *Dualism*. It is proposed

to be an inherently more metaphysically imbalanced such approach toward mental (or cerebral) methodologies and systems given *nondual* awareness has before been described as an extremely basic (or primordial) sort of consciousness, thereby is considered such a philosophical approach particularly modelled, programmed, or mapped to aid (or to help guide one toward) the formation and development of a more *nondual* (or imbalanced) psychological shape, state, or condition of one's mentality (or within one's conscious awareness); while such *nondual* electrochemical incorporation and pattern development is proposed, as aforesaid, exceedingly more preferred by a typical elitist-mindset—given such *nondual* seeking is speculated to somehow be connected to an excessive desire to electrochemically disengage such burdensome connection to the human conscience—versus (or comparatively to) as much being sought after by an individual *journeying along* (discussed below) an existential path while generally in pursuit of a more metaphysically balanced (or *dual*) such state, shape, or condition of one's mentality (or within one's conscious awareness).

NOTE: that such said *"journeying along"* metaphysically tends to involve a more conscious working toward increasingly becoming aware (or increasingly mindful) of the affect that BOTH metaphysical polarities (or cosmic *duality of force*) may seek to persuade upon/within an individual, and whilst comparatively contrasted against a more *nondual* such path, map, or approach, it's proposed that the prior (or the more *dual*) path, map, or approach is more characterized by:

- greater metaphysical challenge given the constant pursuing of higher degrees of spiritual enlightenment while accompanied by, even fuelled by, the foreknowledge and acceptance that certain sought-to-be-answered questions may never reach such fate within any sort of absolutist context
- a relatively greater openminded approach towards various sorts and forms of communication and competition
- a more resolute personal affirmation that there exists potential omnipresent danger within any sort of more absolutist (or *nondual*) doctrine, creed, or metaphysical approach; whilst (as previously discussed) it's proposed that the psychological state, shape, or condition of *Dualism* trumps that of *nondualism* in terms of effectively aiding the internal maintenance of an electrochemical connection between a human's conscience and such related affects upon the individual's body

3. For the purposes of this book, Plotinus is an important philosophical figure given his founding

of Neoplatonism within the Roman Empire—
as so later-deemed by 19ᵗʰ century historians—
where Plotinus found such success within both
Eastern and Western divisions of the empire
wherein, at minimum, as much proves that leading
Roman elitists (within such pagan culture) found
metaphysical value in Platonic philosophy whilst
populous Christianity was concurrently spreading
throughout the Byzantine citizenry (person to
person) during the many decades prior to certain
elitist Byzantine societal-controllers eventually
deeming it necessary for their empire to publicly
convert to Christianity.

NOTE: that more discussion concerning the Byzantine
(Roman) Empire is found further along within this
book, including discussion concerning how such sorts
of Byzantine elitists deemed it intelligent (or advisable)
to slaughter St. George relatively soon before publicly
declaring Christianity more tolerable by state edict

4. The Neoplatonic principle concerning THE ONE
   is an integral term, idea, or premise as well within
   Hermetical doctrine and philosophy.
5. Marsilio Ficino was born and died (1433—1499
   AD/CE) within the Republic of Florence—being
   of territory under the sway of the House of Medici.
   Ficino was a Renaissance scholar and priest within
   Catholicism, and he inevitably became renown as
   an integral figure within an intellectual calling
   (of sorts) to reintroduce both *Hermeticism* and

Neoplatonism (later to be coined as such) back to Europe whilst Ficino—considered as having been heavily under the directive influence of the House of Medici—was the first to translate, from Greek to Latin, historically important portions of both Plato's original manuscripts, and portions of the ancient *Hermetica* [essentially considered as being a Hermetical bible (of sorts)] including the portion more specifically referred to as the *Corpus Hermeticum*. Ficino, in time, also served as a tutor and a teacher respectively to Lorenzo de' Medici and Giovanni Pico della Mirandola; wherein the subjects studied are proposed to have involved discussion regarding the elitist philosophy pertaining to both Neoplatonism and *Hermeticism*.

6. Giovanni Pico della Mirandola (1463—1494 AD/CE) was born in Mirandola, Italy (close to Florence) and inevitably died in Florence; meanwhile Leonardo da Vinci was born within the same regions of Northern Italy in 1452.

During the course of Mirandola's and Da Vinci's respective lives, both men spent time studying and working within Florence and Venice while (perhaps at differing times) having had the same patron (or employer) in the House of Medici, whereby it should be difficult to imagine that Mirandola and Da Vinci didn't establish some sort of relationship; while what sort of influence one had upon the other would seem to be more of a speculative nature.

Mirandola eventually became recognized for his expert knowledge within the philosophical worlds of both *Hermeticism* and Neoplatonism. Much of such keen knowledge is proposed to have been gained whilst studying at the University of Padua within the Venetian region of Italy; the University of Padua being a very historically important institutional bastion for the study of *Hermeticism* within Renaissance Europe.

NOTE: that the University of Padua is proposed as a historically important institution, as well, as per enabling Western Esotericism to blossom within Renaissance Europe, as will be further discussed within this book https://en.m.wikipedia.org/wiki/Western_esotericism

The following quote was selected from within a Wikipedia article titled *Giovanni Pico della Mirandola*: https://en.m.wikipedia.org/wiki/Giovanni_Pico_della_Mirandola

> (He) was an Italian Renaissance nobleman and philosopher[14]...He is famed for the events of 1486, when at the age of 23, he proposed to defend 900 theses on religion, philosophy, natural philosophy, and magic against all comers, for which he wrote the Oration on the Dignity of Man, which has been called the "Manifesto

---

[14] *"Pico della Mirandola, Giovanni, Conte"* in *Grolier Encyclopedia of Knowledge*, volume 15 (Grolier Inc., 1991).

of the Renaissance",[15] and a key text of Renaissance humanism and of what has been called the "Hermetic Reformation".[16]

...Pico was introduced to the mystical Hebrew Kabbalah, which fascinated him, as did the late classical Hermetic writers, such as Hermes Trismegistus. The Kabbalah and Hermetica were thought in Pico's time to be as ancient as the Old Testament.[17]

...In the Oratio de hominis dignitate (Oration on the Dignity of Man, 1486), Pico justified the importance of the human quest for knowledge within a Neoplatonic framework. The Oration also served as an introduction to Pico's 900 theses, which he believed to provide a complete and sufficient basis for the discovery of all knowledge, and hence a model for mankind's ascent of the chain of being. The 900 Theses are a good example of humanist syncretism, because Pico combined Platonism, Neoplatonism, Aristotelianism, Hermeticism and Kabbalah.

---

[15] *Oration on the Dignity of Man* (1486) wsu.edu Archived 4 January 2011 at the Wayback Machine.
[16] James D. Heiser, *Prisci Theologi and the Hermetic Reformation in the Fifteenth Century* (Malone, TX: Repristination Press, 2011).
[17] J. H. (Yossi) Chajes and Yuval Harari, *"Practical Kabbalah: Guest Editor's Introduction"* (Aries: 2 January 2019), 19 (1): 1–5.

They also included 72 theses describing what Pico believed to be a complete system of physics. Mirandola's De animae immortalitate (Paris, 1541), and other works, developed the doctrine that man's possession of an immortal soul freed him from the hierarchical stasis. Pico may have believed in universal reconciliation, since one of his 900 theses was "A mortal sin of finite duration is not deserving of eternal but only of temporal punishment"[18]

.... In the *Oration* he argues, in the words of Pier Cesare Bori, that "human vocation is a mystical vocation that has to be realized following a three stage way, which comprehends necessarily moral transformation, intellectual research and final perfection in the identity with the absolute reality. This paradigm is universal, because it can be retraced in every tradition."[19]

Mirandola was apparently obsessive about encouraging a public synthesis of Christian Kabbalah (proposed basically as synonymous with Esoteric Christianity),

---

[18] *"Apocatastasis"*, *New Schaff-Herzog Encyclopedia of Religious Knowledge*, *Vol. I.*
[19] Prof. Pier Cesare Bori, *The Italian Renaissance: An Unfinished Dawn?: Pico della Mirandola* Archived 29 December 2007 at the Wayback 2007-12-05. Machine. Accessed.

Hermeticism, and Neoplatonism, as Pico perhaps felt these 3 philosophical approaches had adequate (or sufficient) elitist congruence concerning their respective applicability toward (or within) *Mentalism* and *Metaphysics* (terms defined in Chapter 1). https://en.m.wikipedia.org/wiki/Christian_Kabbalah

https://en.m.wikipedia.org/wiki/Esoteric_Christianity

Pico aged only 31 years whereby arsenic poisoning is considered a likely cause of his death.

Pico apparently was a fiery orator that could command an audience of enthralled listeners. This indeed could've largely contributed to Pico's death being so hastened where (or when) if he would've continuously surrendered to possible internal compulsions to publicly speak impassioned on *certain learned knowledge* (discussed below) then, thereby, Pico may've been destined to irrevocably ruffle some excessively paranoid elitist feathers-of-neuroses.

NOTE: that said *"certain learned knowledge"* could've been of the sort of knowledge that historically, more esoterically, remained shrouded within so-called 'secretive societies'—including within those considered internal to the Vatican—of *certain knowledge*, at least in part, that Pico is proposed to have learned whilst studying at the University of Padua

Upon working to properly consider the body of Pico's cumulative efforts invested toward public speaking (or presentations), he may've considered such related efforts of an enlightened (or enlightening) intentionality while perhaps working to make such usually-shrouded knowledge more publicly known and understood; possibly of efforts, fuelled by supportive rationales, wherein Pico may've personally determined his intentionality as of something that could've manifested in helpful ways while having the benefit of populace concern within the forefront of his mind.

The House of Medici, within its core, has before been speculated (or suspected) as being essentially of so-called 'secretive society'; incidentally 4 members of the Medici family were respectively selected to serve as the Catholic pope during/within the 16th and 17th centuries.

Pico was known to have been quite familiar with the Medici—namely Lorenzo de' Medici. Pico allowed himself to become involved in a romantic affair with a woman related to Lorenzo de' Medici, while Lorenzo (at times) was said to have worked to protect Pico from potential associated reprisal.

Hermeticism (back to the discussion…)

Hermeticism is proposed to be a *power theism* of certain principles and doctrine whereby the more such is religiously practiced (or habitually observed) then the more likely it's considered that such a practitioner's brain receives a sort of compounding psychological, mental, or cerebral encouragement (or instigation) to cut off its electrochemical-patterned-development to exclude any sort of related affects associable to the right hemisphere of brain.

Thereby, within such a scenario, a *woefully unenlightening* (discussed below) psychological process is proposed to occur wherein a human's body (over time) becomes increasingly conditioned to experience diminished electrochemical affects associated to the right hemisphere of brain.

NOTE: that such an 'illuminated' psychological process is proposed as so *"woefully unenlightening"* granted consideration for that the right hemisphere of brain is theorized to be the region, area, or hemisphere of brain which possesses the potentiality for an individual's body to maintain electrochemical connection with the individual's conscience

Such a Dark psychological process is proposed to increase the chances that such an increasingly conditioned Hermetical brain—through a *Mental Alchemical* process—may hazardously (or desperately) normalize a spiritual perspective revolving around the premise that such a *power theism* should be viewed as of divine creed.

This proposed premise could explain why ONLY the Vitruvian Man's head (and not his main body) was drawn, by Leonardo da Vinci, to tilt towards the right half (or hemisphere) of the large circle within the Vitruvian Man schematic once the large circle has been dissected, vertically down its centre line, into a *duo* of equal sized halves (or hemispheres).

Perhaps as much can also explain for why Leonardo da Vinci drew Vitruvian Man's LEFT EYE to look much DARKER than his right eye.

Incidentally Hermes's Caduceus can (depending on the artist's depiction) offer the superimposed perimeter outline of an inverted Equilateral Triangle (as this can be independently verified within various artistic depictions of the Caduceus found on the internet); being the same shape, state, or condition (of an inverted congruency to) of the Equilateral Triangle which Da Vinci shaded to surround Vitruvian Man's LEFT EYE.

Within attempts to consider all things, the theory contends that the preceding fact shouldn't be hastily dismissed as simple coincidence without some sort of consideration for the reality that Hermes's Caduceus is an ancient pagan symbol of which Da Vinci would've likely been aware of whilst possibly, simultaneously, having grown wary of such considered-to-be identifiable potential dangers (as previously proposed to exist within *Hermeticism*) related to its habitual (or religious) observation and practice (including such related possible concerns for the associated *Mental Alchemical* element within the doctrine).

Was as much part of a message of hope? Of warning? Or of simple observation shrouded within the Vitruvian Man schematic?

Perhaps Leonardo drew ONLY the head portion of Vitruvian Man while working within the Leaning Tower of Pisa?

The theory contends that Leonardo da Vinci, one way or another, would've likely established a certain awareness of *Hermeticism* given the theism's estimated significance within Renaissance Italy. And while also estimating that Leonardo was most likely a man of conscience, then such established awareness would've likely come along with some sort of recognition of the cunning trappings and potential dangers proposed to exist as per this spiritually unbalancing ancient creed.

Such dangerous potentiality, proposed as existent within *Hermeticism*, may involve a latent bewildering desire—and/or some sort of ultimate mystifying goal, possibly associated to an 'illuminated' spellbinding charm and seeking—incessantly burning to cast *Mental Alchemically* induced spells over entire worldly populations whereby masses of people could become aligned mentally (or electrochemically) congruent with how certain controlling-elitists already are so aligned.

NOTE: that said "induced spells" would be proposed of a sort considered to exist shrouded within the intellectual (or philosophical) instruction and practice, of (and for) the Dark mental arts, as per such related Hermetical teachings

Could the proposed preceding narrative serve to assist any sort of genuine effort in seeking a realistic explanation for why it is that Hermes's Caduceus eventually became an institutionalized symbol for the practice of modern medicine?

If one chooses to seriously contemplate the above query, then perhaps it is advisable to consider that many citizens of various nations, across the world, suspect that their respective populations are currently becoming beguiled (consciously or otherwise) within a seeming slithering (or serpentine) sort of procession toward falling entrapped within some sort of pit (or depression) of a medicalized form of tyranny.

It's proposed as worthy to note that this current massive sort of beguilement seems characterized, at least in part, by the so-called 'mass media' provoking public calls for the imposition of excessively stringent institutional order upon populations assessed to currently (resultantly, to such provocations) contain increasingly large-scale development of mass groupings of brain (or brain activity) melds (or such melding) of a seeming *groupthink mentality.*

Such increases in the development of *groupthink mentality* seem to have been psychologically prodded (or at least encouraged) by an apparent massive (synergistic)

institutional suggestion to do so—thereby considerably adding to a perplexing social pressure that may, somehow (consciously or otherwise), be Darkly enchanting for increases in fear-soaked emotional energies that are proposed to naturally (or electrochemically) serve to aid in the promotion, fostering, and sustainment of the normalization of polarized (thusly polarizing) social climates, which all together, sadly may be forcing people (as per individually devised means to mentally survive) toward antithetical (or extremely opposing) ends of so many debated issues that concern and press upon a society.

NOTE: that certain citizens (within preceding scenario) can increasingly find themselves associating with higher levels of *groupthink mentality* [meaning as being contributory parts of such psychological arenas wherein the siren call of stigma (if you will) is possibly signalling from the metaphysical Darkness, with increasing intensity, while perhaps working to seduce (as per obscure sorts of ways) for its own detonation as a social weapon (or tool) to be cast, invoked, or parlayed within efforts to have 'their side' win]

Furthermore, a particular 'glow' relating to said *"groupthink mentality"* seems to exist inside the cerebral nucleus (or at least existing inside the idea of such a thing) at the center of a polarized (or antithetical) end (or opposing side; thusly offering an extreme parameter) to a certain currently pressing societal issue whereby such a proposed 'glow', ironically, may be serving to dim (or diminish) such associative abilities to compassionately cognate whilst truly desiring (or internally burning; in so many words) to remain objective (or open-minded) given that such particular *groupthink* narratives presently profess it preposterous to even entertain a shadow-of-a-notion that a fraction-of-a-chance could possibly (even potentially) exist—amidst currently developing societal scenarios— wherein some sort of *fascistic synergy* (discussed below) could somehow (consciously or otherwise) be growing within (or may eventually bloom resultant to) present-day public (or civil) evolutions (or degradations) associated to covid as it pertains to such related massive institutional response and approach; whereupon, somehow, governments and corporations clearly are increasingly melding (or morphing) their respective future path's together (for good or bad) thereby proposed as projecting to increase the scope of sway for all institutions involved.

Meanwhile, the truth is that such said *"fascistic synergy"* may eventually prove to be currently fuelling such titanic institutional response and approach from within the core of such a massive collaboration of organizational efforts. However, if such is the case, as much may only be possible to properly identify upon such a proposed monstrous force potentially rearing its head—of a conceptualized absolutist force of societal control—once such related dust settles.

Within efforts to apply open-minded (or objective) consideration to all such relating narratives, perhaps it becomes appropriate to pose the following question:

If such mass groupings of brain (or brain activity) observe (consciously or otherwise) the Hermetic Caduceus—particularly under a banner, flag, or symbol of medicine—does as much have any sort of significant mental, psychological, or cerebral affect (or effect) relating to a potential Alchemical conditioning of a population?

ADDITIONAL NOTE ONE

The theory contends that ancient *Hermeticism* (one way or another) has always been cloaked within the Church because of a Roman infusion (nascently or protractedly) of their longtime-trusted Paganism (identified as *Hermeticism*, as per the theory brought forth within this book) by way of their sponsoring, custodial, and institutional, influence upon Christianity.

As much is argued as a valid proposal whilst considering that Ancient Greco-Roman Hermetical doctrine could've continued to be observed (or practiced) by such elitist social-controllers—pulled back away from the public eye—to within some ancient forms of so-called 'secretive societies' thereby, naturally, creating a type of *Dual public-private model* for institutional structure and system for how to manage, govern, or lead a citizenry within society.

Such ancient forms of so-called 'secretive societies' are proposed as likely to have formed within the Byzantine (Roman) Empire's inner core of controlling-elitists.

The following 3 listed events (or such historical points in time) would've then (within such a narrative and scenario) been part of an *elaborate process* (proposed to include said nascent and protracted stages) involved as per the creation and establishment of the Byzantine Empire's particularly fashioned *Dual public-private model* for such institutional structure and system:

NOTE: that such an *"elaborate process"* is proposed to have most likely initiated upon such controlling-elitists eventually becoming overwhelmed by an impetus to do as much wherein such associated stimulation may've been mainly spurred by a dramatic sort of desperate seeking for realistic means and ways (or for some sort of synthesized solution) capable of supporting the continuance of their assumed beloved Paganism whilst (concurrently) the philosophical, spiritual, and/or metaphysical populace world around them was seemingly amidst some sort of metamorphosis; hence such elitists' eventual discernment that it was necessary to establish such proposed *Dual public-private model* for institutional governance of societal systems and structure

- the Edict of Milan (313 AD/CE), instituted as the Roman Empire's first major public sympathies enacted for Christians
- the Council of Nicaea (325 AD/CE), being the first substantial institutional effort to create a consensus church within the Roman Empire
- the Edict of Thessalonia (380 AD/CE), making Christianity the state religion of the Roman

Empire thereby authorizing the persecution of Christian creeds and interpretations not approved by the Church

Concerning the audacious metaphysical, and physical, venture for massively powerful institutions to widescale orchestrate the development of optimal approaches and strategies for the formation, adoption, and administration of major populace theisms—which are proposed to always inevitably involve (consciously or otherwise) consideration for certain *Mental Alchemical* affects (and effects) upon a people—such undertakings clearly are enormously complex in scale and scope wherewith are typically drawn-out, and play out, over generational measures-of-time.

And, over time, just as the *Word of Socrates* (to coin a phrase) could be massaged and managed toward a more interpretative view—guided by Plato—so could the *Word of Christ* (while coining) be managed and bent toward the will and situational interpretations of the Church; of such situational interpretations many times dependent upon whatever circumstances such institutional leaders could find themselves within intellectualizing (or conceptualizing) during when various extreme (or polarized) political climates can create a sort of pressurized environment that [while within spiritually weakened *nondual* (or gonzo elitist) shapes, states, or conditions] can blind metaphysically, bound legally, and bind socially.

In other words, a people may naturally have a greater inherent ability—over time—to more accurately remember and recall the true vibe and tenure of populace metaphysical messaging, principles, and doctrine better than any associated ability inherent within the nature of massive institutions; whereas massive institutions are proposed to possess a general intrinsic interest in the tailoring (even moulding) of any such populace memory, recall, or interpretations more toward any particular massive institution's will, agenda, or associative elitist ideations.

The theory contends that certain so-called 'secretive societies' of Western Esotericism (as aforementioned) have historically maintained themselves within *Dual public-private models* (of a proposed sort) whereby the members of such a 'society' are proposed to find great intelligence in publicly draping themselves within the more openly accepted Catholicism and/or Christianity whilst privately more observing and practicing the principles and rituals of the ancient Hermetical creed; while such *Dual public-private model* most likely founded their roots within the Byzantine (Roman) Empire, as aforesaid.

The fact is that such grand Paganism-to-Christianity public conversion was of a decades long process, of a final edict of public conversion that was preceded by about 300 years of a populous spreading of such *Word of Christ* among individuals (namely the struggling masses) within the Byzantine (or Roman) controlled lands.

NOTE: that said proposed "populous spreading of such *Word of Christ*" was provided meaning to refer to a certain metaphysical spreading of a more truly open (or populist) ideal of Christianity, whereas such spread was concurrently endeavoured to be quelled by such elitist ruling-Byzantines (even after such gonzo Byzantines apparently deemed it necessary to slaughter St. George—in 303 AD/CE—within told efforts to prevent such then-further spread)
https://en.m.wikipedia.org/wiki/Saint_George

Within an analytical framework of working to study, consider, and understand recorded historical occurrence, the reason for such occurrence, and resultant events to such occurrence, such efforts have been applied toward attempting to keenly discern what sort of intentionality such controlling-elitist Byzantines were truly led by in initiating such public Pagan-to-Christian conversion upon the centuries of witnessing the *Word of Christ* spreading among the dominion of lands associated to their empire-of-control.

Resultant to the application of such a particular analytical process, it is proposed (or discerned) that the Roman Byzantines may've seriously considered as much to be of the *True Word and Wisdom of the Creator* (in coining) whereby, within such a contemplative scenario, the Byzantines perhaps could've determined (or discerned) it wise to more publicly align with the Christian (or Abrahamic) theism while simultaneously pulling back—toward the shadowy ecosystems of more secretive (or esoteric) 'society'—the associative public practices and more open-observation of their traditional Paganism (or *Hermeticism*) whereupon, resultantly, naturally pitting this *duo* of polarities-of-theism against one another within the structure of said institutional *Dual public-private model* for governance and system.

The preceding depicted scenario is indeed proposed as a possible phenomenal occurrence, and given the fact that there exists more esoteric, cloaked, or shrouded approaches to Christianity—such as Esoteric Christianity and Christian Kabbalism (being such Darker philosophies that are suspected to reside at the center of Western Esotericism, and at the core of certain kindred spirited so-called 'secretive societies')—that such more 'secretive' approaches to Christianity may run downstream of (or perhaps exist derivatively resultant to) the aforesaid original/ancient Pagan pullback (by such Byzantines) as per the foundation, establishment, and protraction of said *Dual-modelled structure* for enabling theistic competition to have possibly been set up within the Church; whereby, within such a proposed setting, Byzantine/Roman Paganism (or *Hermeticism*) is proposed to have been sort of SET UP thereby POISED TO COMPETE [from within such esoteric (more closeted) 'societal' (or social) ecosystems] AGAINST the more publicly open populace ideal of Christianity held within such said *Word of Christ*.

ADDITIONAL NOTE TWO

Once the Edict of Thessalonia was authorized in 380 AD/ CE, thereby making Christianity the state religion of the Roman Empire (thusly authorizing the persecution of all religious interpretations not approved by the then-newly founded Church), the Byzantine Empire proceeded then to expand its authority upon land and territory, under its military conquest and domain, to inevitably reach its peak size—in around 555 AD/CE—whereupon their militant empire institutionally controlled practically all the lands surrounding the Mediterranean Sea; whereas (contrastingly) Jesus Christ was said to be of a Peace- advising Abrahamic creed.

Muhammad is said to have been born in 570 AD/CE within Mecca (Saudi Arabia) during a time when the Byzantine Empire had established control over lands which pushed upon the edge of the modern-day Saudi Arabian border.

Muhammad was of an Arabian people that, prior to 570 AD/CE, surely had experienced the stretch of Byzantine military authority and impressing power. It's proposed that Muhammad, along with his people, eventually became convinced and determined that they could unite and discern the interpretations of a militant Abrahamic Peace-advising god as good, or better, than such oppressing Byzantines.

Such narrative can be interpreted to mean that Muhammad may've rationalized that he (and his people) could trump such Byzantine weaponization (or polarization) of Abrahamic theistic philosophy parlayed into empire-building whilst simultaneously of the *dual consideration* that the founding of an Islamic creed can possibly be conceptualized as a reasonable-reaction-of-counteroffensive-strategy given the assumption that such Arabian peoples had most likely previously (before the formation of Islam) suffered significantly under the Byzantine tyranny and sword, drawn-out over time, as such scenarios may've occurred in the flesh.

Islamic militant empires rose and fell around the Mediterranean Sea between the 6th and 20th centuries.

Once a militant Islam was established—proposed as being of a certain congruence to the militant Christian Byzantine Empire—the all-encompassing theism evidently went forward finding comparable temporal success (to that of Byzantines before) within the weaponization of Abrahamic theism and doctrine; while not so ironically (in a sense of living and dying by the sword), militant Islamic armies sacked the Roman Byzantine capital city (Constantinople) in 1453 AD/CE, and then converted it to the then-new capital city of the Islamic Ottoman Empire, renamed Istanbul.

Many Islamic scholars, of Islam's so-called *Golden Age* (said to have occurred between the 8th and 14th centuries), revered and studied the Ancient Greek elitist philosophy of Plato (later coined Neoplatonism) and that of Aristotle; as Plato and Aristotle had both philosophically supported slavery within society thereby beckoning the metaphysical hallmarks and intellectual insignias of typical gonzo elitist character and mentality for how to morally approach, and ideally envision, class-structure for society.

Various strains of intellectual elitism are proposed as much more likely to manifest and develop resultant to excessive (or imbalanced) degrees of observation, practice, and loyalty of (or toward) any variety of elitist interpretations of any sort of theistic philosophy; wherein the argument for slavery being possible to view as a morally tenable class within society perhaps always seems more reasonable and intelligent (whether or not it has been made illegal w/in a society) once such elitist-minded social-controllers begin Darkly weighing the economic benefit of essentially free labour.

The preceding analysis is considered as further argumentative support for a reasonable suspicion that Plato and Aristotle excessively (sycophantically) revered the state-controlled Ancient Greco Pagan gods. These two men would've likely comported themselves as so, at minimum, because they weren't as truly brave as was Socrates (as Socrates was/is historically renown for his courage and fearlessness) while working under the assumption that neither Plato, nor Aristotle, had the stomach as did Socrates in terms of staying true to one's Self.

NOTE: that Aristotle went on (in the flesh) to personal tutor the excessively murderous Alexander the 'Great' whereas Socrates had no time for such state-controlled Greek gods; being such state-controllable *power deities* that Alexander apparently learned how to optimally embrace and parlay within the Macedonian's shot at internationally spreading such 'Word' amidst their savagely plundering campaigns of terror and tyranny

Such logic-based assertions, upon the truer nature of Plato and Aristotle, are extrapolated to propose a contention that these 2 men...at minimum...revered conceptualizations (or idolizations) of Zeus and his son Hermes...whereas beyond minimum...were devoted (or practicing) Hermeticists; while perhaps useful here to recall is that *Hermeticism* and Neoplatonism (perhaps not so coincidentally) practically travelled forward together—over at least the past 1,700 years—as if intellectually hand-in-glove, proposed to be philosophically (or even possibly metaphysically) interlinked with one another.

ADDITIONAL NOTE THREE

Of a certain historical interest, alive during the same period of time were the following men:

- the infamous Niccolò Machiavelli
- the treacherous King Henry VIII
- 3 'holy men' proposed to have significantly influenced King Henry VIII, as per a Hermetic

appeal and attraction, in Thomas Starkey, Reginald Pole, and Francesco Zorzi/Giorgi (the 'holy man' with two last names)

- Leonardo da Vinci (of Vitruvian Man creation) and Giovanni Pico della Mirandola (being the afore-detailed Hermetic-and-Neoplatonic impassioned one)

NOTE: that John Dee (1527—1608 AD/CE) was the next generation of apparent Hermetic masters; John Dee being the occult Hermetic teacher, and high spiritual advisor, to Queen Elizabeth I (daughter of King Henry VIII)

Niccolò Machiavelli (1469—1527 AD/CE) was born in Florence, Italy and "has often been called the father of modern political philosophy and political science".[20]

Leonardo da Vinci (1452—1519 AD/CE) was born in Vinci, Italy (close to Florence).

Giovanni Pico della Mirandola (1463—1494 AD/CE)— as previously discussed—was born in Mirandola, Italy (close to Florence), and inevitably died in Florence. Giovanni became renown for his mastery of knowledge associated to *Hermeticism* and Neoplatonism. He studied at the University of Padua; being the Venetian regional institution important for Hermetic education (as is further discussed within this section of the book). https://en.m.wikipedia.org/wiki/University_of_Padua

---

[20] Frederick G. Whelan, *Hume and Machiavelli: Political Realism and Liberal Thought* (Lexington Books, 2004), *29*.

Thomas Starkey (1498—1538 AD/CE), Reginald Pole (1500—1558 AD/CE) and Francesco Zorzi/Giorgi (1466—1540 AD/CE) became historically important, in the way that they did, by way of their direct associations with King Henry VIII; while these 3 'holy men' also will be discussed in further detail within this section of the book.

The telling of the stories (in part) of King Henry VIII and these 3 'holy men' is proposed as useful (or valuable) for the purposes of adding context to the theory brought forth throughout this book.

Associatively, a contention is offered arguing that the advisory support of these 3 'holy men' was very important for Henry VIII to gain a Hermetical knowledge, and a related necessary confidence, to turn England against the impositions of the Catholic Church.

The fact is that these 3 'holy men' were not only steeped in the ways of Catholicism, but also became learned in *Hermeticism* through their respective amounts of time spent immersed within its study whilst attending the University of Padua. It's proposed that upon such a more complete Hermetic realization that Henry may've concluded that he could potentially make a historic bold decision, cut off ties with the Catholic Church, and simply push ahead better with England's own Abrahamic interpretation (and rule) under an Anglican Church.

The University of Padua is the aforesaid Venetian-based historically important institution which largely enabled the Hermetic doctrine to be carried forward, into Renaissance Europe, from centuries prior.

The University of Padua is proposed to have become of much greater situational relevance (in terms of serving as a prime location for Hermetic teaching) once the Byzantine Constantinople fell to the Ottomans in 1453 AD/CE.

The University of Padua is proposed to have become an immensely significant institution, within a *modern esoteric sense* (discussed below), due to the British Empire's ultimate global success; while not possible, in the way as much occurred, without the foundation of the BRIC (British East India Company, founded in 1600). https://en.m.wikipedia.org/wiki/East_India_Company

NOTE: that within a proposed *"modern esoteric sense"* is stated as so as to highlight the limited contemporary (or 21st century) populace understanding of *Hermeticism's* 16th century influence and affect upon important geopolitical developments and occurrences; including for how *Hermeticism* is proposed to have travelled along a path, from Venice to London, destined to infiltrate King Henry VIII's inner-circles via the human conduction of (at least by) the 3 aforesaid 'holy men' (whom had received such Hermetic education at the Venetian-regional University of Padua); which will all be further discussed within this section

Incidentally the Venetian Empire, prior to the 16th century, had accrued centuries of experience within a cutthroat blend of seafaring war-and-commerce led by its Venetian Navy; the Venetian Navy being a suitable predecessor model for the BRIC to emulate—wherein such commerce largely involved the classically gonzo elitist trade for slaves, while the Republic of Venice had also then-previously banked centuries of experience within the craft of *money changing.*
https://en.m.wikipedia.org/wiki/Venetian_navy

https://en.m.wikipedia.org/wiki/Money_changer

NOTE: that Paul Warburg—of 20th century banking fame as a co-founding interest within the Federal Reserve System—was considered of a Venetian family of expert money changing knowledge and pedigree whereby "The Warburg family is thought to have originated from Venice, at which point they bore the surname *del-Banco.*"[21]
https://en.m.wikipedia.org/wiki/Warburg_family

The 3 'holy men'—listed and discussed below (and more deeply discussed within the pages to follow)—all spent historically important amounts of time studying at the Venetian-regional University of Padua:

NOTE: that these 3 'holy men' are assumed to have directly influenced Henry VIII toward embracing and

[21] Ron Chernow, *The Warburgs: The Twentieth Century Odyessy of a Remarkable Jewish Family* (New York: Random House, 1993), 3–5.

enveloping such *Hermeticism* by, and within, Henry's inner-rings and English royal court—thereby proposed to have aided in the provision of a foundation for the development and growth of Western Esotericism within Anglicized culture; including to help foster development of a cultural (or societal) foundation for particular so-called 'secretive societies' to quasi-esoterically establish themselves within Early Modern Britain, such as those associated to Freemasonry and of Rosicrucianism

1. Reginald Pole was an English cardinal of the Roman Catholic Church who, separately, spent years of time studying at the University of Padua
2. Thomas Starkey studied at the University of Padua between 1521 to 1526; he was known as a close associate to Reginald Pole
3. Francesco Zorzi (Giorgi), who may've been the most significant of the various Padua-educated 'holy men' to have so significantly (in a historical sense) influenced King Henry VIII

The stories of these 3 'holy men' connect Renaissance Venice to King Henry VIII's England. Their stories also are proposed as associable evidence that various Venetian elitists eventually became of a particular rationalized interest-of-despair (as discussed below) to directly inspire and influence a Venetian-styled metamorphosis within England—initially by way of winning over hearts and minds of Anglo fellow elitists who had already established themselves within Henry's inner-rings and English royal court—within a hopeful vision of encouraging and guiding London toward eventually morphing into becoming of a city-state model (as had, then, already been made successful within the city-states of Venice, Rome, Genoa, and Florence) so as to create a suitable cultural foundation, and necessary socioeconomic infrastructure, that if London did inevitably seek to geopolitically emerge upon the world scene as a supermassive juggernaut of global-domineering success, then as much could've at least been set up to more swiftly occur in such case; which is indeed of the path that Britain obviously inevitably chose to pursue through its British-particular blend of seafaring war-and-commerce (of such a model that had then-previously been mastered, during and within those prior centuries, by such similarly ocean-bound fellow elitists of the city-state Republic of Venice).

However, under what set of circumstances could possibly position such excessively self-serving elitist Venetians wherein they could find themselves rationalizing it necessary (or intelligent) to help Henry VIII within any means at all?

That query will be approached next.

King Henry VIII

In Henry looking for support from the Catholic Church to divorce his then-wife Catherine of Aragon (a Spanish princess), as much added to a list of circumstances proposed to have 'set the stage' for *Hermeticism* to not only flourish within the more elitist societal classes of Renaissance England, but also added to the likelihood that *Hermeticism* could increasingly spread and succeed more globally; ironically while Shakespeare was figurately warming up his ink-dipped feather.

A successful global spreading of *Hermeticism* is proposed to have been necessarily dependant upon the establishment of strong grips of loyalty to develop within the hearts and minds of possibly prospecting (for whatever particular reason) Hermeticists, from around the world, from within the various nations of then-current, or then-future, *British incorporation*; of such a proposal while working to simultaneously reconcile the notion that Elitism is Elitism, no matter the corner of the world, whilst *Hermeticism* seems to globally (or transnationally) fit the bill as it is of a universal-styled doctrine.

NOTE: that such said *"British incorporation"* may've, as per whatever particular case imaginable, been established by means of either (but not limited to) trade, manipulation, negotiation, entrapment, coercion, blackmail, submission, war, or treaty...as all's fair in love, war, and *Hermeticism*—within metaphysical realms and arenas where fathers develop such strong mental addictions to their perceived power that they would rather murder their own sons than surrender their position atop a family/social hierarchy

The remainder of this section will attempt to detail other circumstances proposed to have significantly contributed to such a setting-of-the-stage for this depicted global Hermetical spread to successfully occur throughout, and within, the various British incorporated power-centres positioned and poised all around the world; whereby one such proposed circumstance was the fact that upon King Henry VIII breaking off his marriage with the Spanish princess, Spain and England then went on to seemingly drive one another to excessively (or Darkly) compete with one another, over time, toward apparent designs on colonizing the entire globe under the control of their respective royal Crowns-of-incorporation. Perhaps all of a Hermetically affiliated dream.

King Henry VIII and the League of Cambria

The *War of the League of Cambria* (1508–1516 AD/ CE)—of a warring period initially launched as per designs to reduce the military and economic scope and sway of the Venetian Empire—occurred as the Republic of Venice (established in 697) had already, by the year 1508, survived about 800 years of the political and religious warring scene of Western Europe, along with having thrived as a military empire-of-commerce during the so-called *Dark Ages*.

Machiavellianism is a political philosophy that congealed within the regions of Northern Italy wherein NOT ONLY the historic political successes of the House of Medici (founded in 1230) assumedly offered Niccolò

Machiavelli much to observe and study, BUT ALSO such regional political stages (during the same time-period) showcased as much within the stratagem of such beguiling Renaissance Venetians—wherein, and whereby, if a 16th century prize had to be presented…to…say…a champion "Machiavellian Outfit Award Winner", then surely these two wickedly conniving Renaissance contenders would've postured fierce contention for such a thing.

The fact is that within the worlds of politics, banking, and international commerce—backed by military strength—typical elitist Venetians had long been generally characterized by such high degrees of devilish guile, artful duplicitousness, and a shrew ruthlessness that the Republic of Venice thusly had infamously (during the course of its empire) abided by such a notorious tone and tenor that it arguably NOT ONLY helped their republic survive into the future, as it had, BUT ALSO to assist its imperial impressing growth when it was pursuing more expansionary military policy.

The *War of the League of Cambria* was most likely mainly conceptualized and spurred into action by gonzo elitists within the Catholic Church looking to supress Venetian authority within Italy, but also such war may have near-gleefully been committed toward by other participating Western nations given the possibility of various built-up resentments toward such Machiavellian Venetians for (such assumed) previous dastardly deeds committed upon, and within, such European stages and worlds.

NOTE: that while on one hand the Catholic Church was telling Henry that it wouldn't recognize his divorce from the Spanish princess, whilst on the other hand the Vatican was an instrumental (or orchestrating) institution within such early 16th century warring efforts devised to rub the Republic of Venice of the Italian political map of influence and sway, whereby, all adding up perhaps to substantively increase the chances that certain future geopolitical developments would ensue (as further detailed below)

In any event, during the *War of the League of Cambria*, such stages witnessed Spain and England teaming-up together—through their shared Catholic bond—against the Republic of Venice for most of the 8-year warring period. Thusly, the Venetian Empire had geopolitically found itself within a desperately vulnerable position.

Upon such realization is when it's estimated that a Venetian elitist brain trust (of sorts) spearheaded action towards devising successful strategies seeking to assure that the Republic of Venice would NOT ONLY survive-and-advance beyond the *War of the League of Cambrai*, BUT ALSO to brainstorm possible ways (or means) to dramatically reduce the probability that such future geopolitical scenarios could develop in where Spain and England could again find themselves joining the same side (or the same warring efforts), against the Republic of Venice, given any potential sets of political circumstance whereby such type war could possibly manifest.

This led to a measured point where such Renaissance Venetians determined it intelligent to set their sights toward seducing, preying upon, and exploiting the flaws-of-excess they'd identified within the character of King Henry VIII.

Within efforts to understand the Machiavellianism within such a thing, such double-dealing Venetians are estimated (roughly) to have determined (upon such a historical point in time) the following:

Given the Spanish Empire's then-great military might—of such an impressing enormity displayed NOT ONLY within the *League of Cambria*'s main efforts to squash the Venetians, BUT ALSO possibly within any potential future *League of Cambria*-type efforts—that if somehow England could've been influenced, manipulated, or guided toward becoming politically turned against Spain…then the Republic of Venice thusly would increase its chances of surviving into the future.

In any event, the eventual result of such related geopolitical developments indeed found the Spanish Empire focusing more on England—and less on the Republic of Venice—as their primary enemy.

Once Henry triggered the divorce, Spain and England became chief warring rivals for each other during those decades to follow.

The Republic of Venice survived until the year 1797.

The premise is that certain members of such proposed Venetian elitist brain trust inevitably (as assumed resultant to such related Dark brainstorming sessions) identified the exploitation of Henry's excessive lust for worldly things as good strategy (or foreign policy)—as per broader devises to ensure the survival of the Republic of Venice into the future—whilst Henry was searching for religious support to divorce Catherine of Aragon (which eventual occurred in 1533).

Within such a premise, Renaissance Venetian elitists are proposed to have identified Henry as a man that could be compromised and captured by a particular Venetian-styled seduction; whereby as much may've ultimately been of the grand tornadic metaphysical suck proposed as perpetually existent within a pulling (or mesmerizing) vortex of machinations and exploitation that can be envisioned to Darkly 'glow' and churn at the center of Hermetical spiritual philosophy and such Pagan hierarchical (or social, political) approach (at least as so depicted while considering certain evidentiary underpinnings, as will be further discussed).

Of the human conduits that could've potentially driven, and managed, such significant influence upon Henry's various philosophical approaches, *men of religion* are estimated to have been the most likely to accomplish as much as such was of the obvious political power structure for 16th century Europe.

Of such certain Venice-influenced 'holy men' (or *men of religion*), who eventually did serve to advise Henry VIII, such 'holy men', within their heart, are proposed to have been (or to have ultimately become) more of Esoteric, Kabbalistic, or gonzo elitist interpretations of Christianity; while such philosophical terms (or approaches), and their associative practices and principles, are proposed to fundamentally fall under an overarching Hermetical creed and doctrine.

The fact is that, since 1527, Henry had publicly appealed to the Catholic Church for approval to annul his marriage to the Spanish princess whilst as much is proposed as the identified grand opportunity (or glaring weakness) upon which the pull of Venice would seek to capitalize.

All such 3 'holy men' are proposed to have been of an expert level of Hermetic education and knowledge resultant to their respective time spent whilst studying at the Venetian-based University of Padua.

The following paragraphs tell of their stories one-by-one, interwoven with details deemed relevant for the purposes of the book.

Reginald Pole (1500—1558 AD/CE)

Reginald Pole was an English cardinal of the Roman Catholic Church.
https://en.m.wikipedia.org/wiki/Reginald_Pole

Reginald Pole studied at the University of Padua for a determined main reason as to learn better of the Hermetic theism and doctrine.

From the above-listed Wikipedia article titled *Reginald Pole*:

> Pole's studies in Padua were partly financed by his election as a fellow of Corpus Christi College, Oxford, with more than half of the cost paid by Henry VIII himself on 14 February 1523, which allowed him to study abroad for three years.[22] [23]

Pole is considered to have prototypically embodied the essence of the following paragraph (which has been copy-and-pasted from the previous section titled "ADDITIONAL NOTE ONE"):

"The theory contends that certain so-called 'secretive societies' of Western Esotericism (as aforementioned) have historically maintained themselves within *Dual public-private models* (of a proposed sort) whereby the members of such a 'society' are proposed to find great intelligence in publicly draping themselves within the more openly accepted Catholicism and/or Christianity

---

[22] *"Lambeth Palace Library Research Guide: Reginald Pole, Archbishop of Canterbury (1500-1558)" (PDF). Lambeth Palace Library. Archived from the original (PDF) on 31 October 2010. Retrieved 16 September 2019.*
[23] Alfred Brotherston Emden, *A biographical register of the University of Oxford, A.D. 1501 to 1540* (Oxford: Clarendon Press, 1974), 453.

whilst privately more observing and practicing the principles and rituals of the ancient Hermetical creed; while such *Dual public-private model* most likely founded their roots within the Byzantine (Roman) Empire, as aforesaid."

Reginald Pole, *publicly*, was a vaunted English Catholic figure for whom Henry strategically desired to support his decision for divorce. More *privately*, Pole studied *Hermeticism* at the Venetian-regional University of Padua, as he did from 1523 to 1526....and then returned to Padua in 1532.

This theoretically made Pole, while cloaked within Catholicism, an ideal man to educate Henry on the creed of *Hermeticism* as Henry was then-just starting to come up with possible solutions to his marital issues whereupon if Henry grew to discover that *Hermeticism* (or Kabbalah Christianity) had always existed shrouded within the Church then as much could've somehow possibly aided to increase Henry's level of confidence within the bold idea (or vision) of possibly leading England toward creating its own such path (or such version) within an Anglican Church.

Henry inevitably offered Reginald Pole the title *Archbishopric of York* perhaps as per some sort of reward in exchange for Pole supporting Henry's final decision to divorce.

Thomas Starkey (1495—1538 AD/CE)

Thomas Starkey, as did Reginald Pole, studied at the University of Padua.
https://en.m.wikipedia.org/wiki/Thomas_Starkey

Thomas Starkey originally had studied at the University of Oxford. After this, by 1523, Starkey found himself within the regions of northern Italy studying at the University of Padua whereby (from the above-listed Wikipedia article titled *Thomas Starkey*):

> (Starkey) went to Padua with Thomas Lupset in 1523. Here he studied the works of Aristotle and admired the government of Venice.[24]

Beyond 1532, Starkey returned to the University of Padua in possible search for to further his Hermetic and Neoplatonic acumen.

Francesco Zorzi/Giorgi (1466—1540 AD/CE)

Francesco Zorzi/Giorgi may be the most significant of the various Padua-educated 'holy men' that influenced Henry within such context.
https://en.m.wikipedia.org/wiki/Francesco_Giorgi

---

[24] *"Starkey, Thomas". Oxford Dictionary of National Biography (online ed.). Oxford University Press. doi:10.1093/ref:odnb/26318.* (Subscription or UK public library membership required.)

Francesco's story is *suitably* shrouded in seeming duplicity; *"suitably"* in that he was indeed a Renaissance Venetian.

In Zorzi's case, for starters, such seeming duplicity appears in reference to the way Wikipedia offers Zorzi's biographical information within two different/unlinked Wikipedia webpages—while one webpage is under the name Francesco Giorgi whereas the other is under the name Francesco Zorzi (wherein the Zorzi-webpage is translated ONLY in French).

Thereby, at least while this book was being finalized, Wikipedia had chopped-up the presentation of Francesco's biographical information on a *duo* of their webpages in a *duo* of languages, unlinked to one another, all within a seeming effort to obfuscate.

But why would such a seeming effort even be considered possibly apparent (or existent)?

Does therein exist conscious effort to conceal the fact that Francesco was Venetian?

If so, then why?

Are we left only to speculate? If so, then we shall...

From within the above-listed Wikipedia article titled *Francesco Giorgi*, we learn that Francesco was "an Italian

Franciscan friar"[25], and that he has some connection to messaging within Shakespeare's *The Merchant of Venice*. Also revealed, from the article, is that Francesco had some association with John Dee (being the occult high-advisor to the daughter of Henry VIII; Elizabeth I), and that historical details concerning Francesco are reviewed comprehensively by Frances Yates within her book *The Occult Philosophy in the Elizabethan Age*.

However, within that relatively short Wikipedia bio—titled *Francesco Giorgi*—no mention is made of either of the facts that he was indeed specifically of a Venetian sort of Italian, nor mention of that he was a historically significant advisor to King Henry VIII; while the later bit of information is offered within the aforesaid unlinked Wikipedia article translated into the language of French, titled *Francesco Zorzi (théologian)*.

Furthermore—as a certain suspicion continued to build—the Wikipedia webpage-bio on Frances Yates (being the aforesaid prolific author on all-things-Zorzi) somehow fails to include mention of the name "Francesco Zorzi (Giorgi)" when discussing the various occult books written by Yates.

From a Wikipedia article titled *Frances Yates*:

---

[25] p. 357. Also (p. 69) the CHRP talks of Giorgi as a synthesizer of the *pia philosophia* of Ficino, and the *concordia* of Giovanni Pico della Mirandola (along with Henricus Cornelius Agrippa and Paracelsus); on p. 312 he is classed with Ficino and Nicolas of Cusa as subscribing to a macrocosm and microcosm theory.

https://en.m.wikipedia.org/wiki/Frances_Yates

In 1941, she was employed by the Warburg Institute, and began to work on what she termed "Warburgian history", emphasising a pan-European and inter-disciplinary approach to historiography. Her most acclaimed publication was *Giordano Bruno and the Hermetic Tradition*(1964), in which she emphasised the role of Hermeticism in Bruno's works and the role that magic and mysticism played in Renaissance thinking. *The Art of Memory* (1966), and *The Rosicrucian Enlightenment* (1972) are also major works. Yates wrote extensively on the occult or Neoplatonic philosophies of the Renaissance, which she is credited with making more accessible.[26]

Why this seeming attempt to obscure?

Or perhaps a more poignant question here to ask is:

Why this seeming attempt to keep such information from people that don't read French?

From the below-listed Wikipedia article titled *Francesco Zorzi (théologian)* the revealing French-sentence is as follows:

---

[26] Marjorie G. Jones, *Frances Yates and the Hermetic Tradition* (Lake Worth, Florida: Ibis Press, 2008), 1.

https://fr.m.wikipedia.org/wiki/Francesco_Zorzi_(théologien)

> Entre 1527 et 1533, Henri VIII d'Angleterre prit contact avec lui, comme nombre de juristes et théologiens, pour étayer sa demande de divorce avec sa première femme Catherine d'Aragon.[27]

This basically translates to:

The theologian (Francesco Zorzi) supported Henry VIII's decision to divorce Catherine of Aragon.

In fact, the French version doesn't even specifically reveal that Zorzi was Venetian, but rather just stated that he was Italian.

Thereby while working under the assumption that it's significant, for the purposes of this book, to document the fact that Francesco Zorzi/Giorgi was in fact specifically Venetian, and not just generally Italian, as much compelled such related search to continue.

Then, alas, stumbled across was a Wikipedia article (unlinked to other such Zorzi/Giorgi Wikipedia articles; at least during when this book was being finalized) titled *Christian Kabbalah* where a certain spilling of such

---

[27] Frances Yates, *La Philosophie occulte à l'époque élisabéthaine* (1979), trad. franç. de Laure de Lestrange, Paris, Dervy-Livres, 1987.

'Venetian beans' (if one will) on Francesco Zorzi was discovered reading:

> Francesco Giorgi, (1467–1540) was a Venetian Franciscan friar and "has been considered a central figure in sixteenth-century Christian Kabbalah both by his contemporaries and by modern scholars". According to Giulio Busi, he was the most important Christian Kabbalist second to its founder Giovanni Pico della Mirandola. His, *De harmonia mundi*, was "a massive and curious book, all Hermetic, Platonic, Cabalistic, and Pinchian"[28]

And within an effort to close on such discussions concerning Francesco Zorzi/Giorgi, the following evidence-of-linkage between Zorsi and Henry VIII (from the British Public Records Office showing direct connection between Zorzi and Henry) whereby such records are discerned as showing Zorzi working, on behalf of Henry, to deny the authority of the Catholic Pope over Henry's marital affairs. Sounds like Francesco Zorzi held some 'holy' institutional sway.

https://books.google.ca/books?id=XiI-AAAAMAA J&pg=PA538&lpg=PA538&dq=francesco+zorzi+hen ry+viii&source=bl&ots=4MDBvcYUAU&sig=NVHx T5cDFZtQIORdclfoT5F8dAI&hl=en&sa=X&ved=0a

---

[28] Don Karr: *The Study of Christian Cabala in English* (pdf), p. 19, accessed on 28 March 2013.

hUKEwifjbGfp5bOAhVnyoMKHUsPD944ChDoA
QhNMA4#v=onepage&q=francesco%20zorzi%20
henry%20viii&f=false

Perhaps is it appropriate here to query whether such analysis truly matters, or not, historically?

If it truly matters, then why all the seeming arcane reporting on Zorzi within Wikipedia's website?

The truth is that Francesco Zorzi may be a very significant historical figure because (in part) there is good chance that Francesco is the central figure of whom Shakespeare had in mind when writing *The Merchant of Venice*, which may curiously be part of the reason why Zorzi is currently (or contemporarily) a barely known elitist Renaissance Venetian of history.

Could any of these previously proposed and discussed narratives have anything to do with why such little open/public discussion ever seems to be institutionally launched directly into the philosophical approach (or the metaphysical world) known as *Hermeticism*?

Could as much have something to do with a proposed premise that *Hermeticism* has always existed within the Church in some shrouded (or esoteric) fashion?

Could such possible concealment have something to do with the fact that Hermes is a mythological son of Zeus, thereby as much directly related to the ideal of a Pagan temporal *power god*?

Could such related institutional neglect be associated to how the modern Westernized world gets the Hermetic Caduceus—of elitist Pagan symbolism—as an international insignia for public health and medicine?

Could it all have something to do with the idea that *Hermeticism* has been at the centre of philosophical principles, practices, and perhaps even religious observation, within a specified model of so-called 'secretive societies' since the Roman Byzantines essentially founded as much as early as within the 4th century AD/CE?

NOTE: that such a "founding" is of the (previously proposed and discussed) premise wherein as much is considered as being of an original/ancient/Byzantine (or Roman Pagan) founding and establishment of such a *Dual public-private modelled* institutional structure and system for how to manage, govern, or lead a citizenry within society

ADDITIONAL NOTE FOUR

This section of the report contains a more complete technical analysis of the Vitruvian Man schematic as it relates to the theory brought forth throughout this book.

The theory could provide insight for why the Equilateral Triangle (or the pyramid shape) is currently, as it was anciently, a major symbol for certain social-engineering elitist interest.

From a proposed *Sacred Geometrical* perspective (or of such a metaphysical approach), the theory contends that such *archetype geometric shapes* (term defined within Chapter 3) can be another manner for how to conceptualize the cross-culturally identified *duality of force* assumed to innately exist within more foundational psychological (or mental) arenas as archetypal form, construct, or pattern, of which likely (somehow) corresponds, transposes, or correlates with (or to) the *duo of polarities* of the cosmos (as detailed within Chapter 1).

NOTE: that aforesaid "another manner for how to conceptualize" is proposed to mean in addition to the more culturally classical linguistic approaches as per such time-tested metaphysical attempts, or spiritual methodologies, designed for how to conceptualize as much; as previously discussed within greater detail, and more tersely summarized below

The theory proposes that the *archetype geometric shape* of the Equilateral Triangle (or the Tetrahedron in 3-D form) geometrically represents the *patterned behavioural shape* of the metaphysical polarity associatively, linguistically, conceptualized as Evil (as per an Ancient Abrahamic approach), Below (as per an Ancient Hermetic approach),

Annihilationism (as per an Ancient Buddhist approach), Yin (as per an Ancient Chinese approach), Dark (as per an historical Native North American approach), and Negative (as per a New Age approach).

Conversely, the theory also proposes that the *archetype geometric shape* of the Circle (or the Sphere in 3-D form) geometrically represents the *patterned behavioural shape* of the metaphysical polarity associatively, linguistically, conceptualized as Good (as per an Ancient Abrahamic approach), Above (as per an Ancient Hermetic approach), Eternalism (as per an Ancient Buddhist approach), Yang (as per an Ancient Chinese approach), Light (as per an historical Native North American approach), and Positive (as per a New Age approach).

As previously detailed, Vitruvian Man's proposed commentary on *Dualism* can clearly be observed contrasting between the man's bodily position in the more Chaotic X pose, versus, the man's bodily position in the more Orderly T pose; whereas Chaos and Order are considered antithetical, paradoxical, or counterbalancing *dual forces* within the same "thing"—in such case the "thing" being the concept of STATE OF BEING.

However, as well aforesaid, some less obvious *dual comparisons* within the Vitruvian Man schematic include:

- the comparatively more Enlightened look of the man's Right eye contrasted against the Darker look of the man's Left eye
- the outlined shape of an Equilateral Triangle shaded to surround the man's Left eye (being of an inverted state, form, or condition) contrasted against the more Circular shape shaded to surround the man's Right eye

Additional Vitruvian Man analysis provides consideration for that if 2 of the 3 most common *archetype geometric shapes*—in the Circle and the Square—are so glaringly visible within the Vitruvian Man schematic (in large-form), then should the question be asked for why the other most common *archetype geometric shape*—in the Equilateral Triangle—is not visibly drawn within the schematic?

In other words, should such a glaring omission be considered part of some sort of riddle presented (or embedded), within the schematic, where observers are subtly (or suggestively) encouraged (by the simple determination of: because one isn't drawn) to hunt for an Equilateral Triangle that could be superimposed (or drawn) upon/within the schematic—in such comparable large-form to that of the Circle and Square already so visibly drawn within the schematic—ultimately within some sort of logical sense or form?

This theory contends affirmative to the idea of such a riddle element being proposed as per the nature and design of the Vitruvian Man schematic. And as it turns out, the only sensible Equilateral Triangle concluded as able to be superimposed (or drawn) upon/within the schematic (to be drawn between any 3 logical connective points within the schematic) is of an *inverted* state (or condition); perhaps not-so-coincidentally just as is the state (or condition) of the Equilateral Triangle—being of an *inverted* state (or condition)—Leonardo da Vinci shaded (or drew) to surround the man's left eye.

NOTE: that all other attempts to draw such a logically forming Equilateral Triangle—that can be drawn between any 3 logical connective points within the schematic—form isosceles triangles

This ONLY Equilateral Triangle able to be superimposed (or drawn) upon/within the Vitruvian Man schematic (while implementing such a logical approach to do so) is one of an *inverted* form wherein its base is formed between the 2 connective points where the man's fingertips are touching the Square (whilst within the T bodily position) where the tip (or the 3rd superimposed connective point) of this *inverted* Equilateral Triangle resides at the centrepoint of the seemingly arbitrary horizontal scoring-line situated beneath the schematic's Square and Circle.

NOTE: that as it applies to the theory brought forth within this book, no other significant reason is determined for that horizontal scoring-line to be provided within the schematic OTHER THAN for the reason of being able to use its centrepoint in order to draw (or superimpose) at least one logically forming *inverted* Equilateral Triangle that matches as much of which Leonardo drew (or shaded) to surround the man's left eye; whereas the observable, seemingly relevant, tick marks on the scoring-line are determined to serve no other significant purpose beyond to appear as potentially significant, at least per the proposed riddle element of the theory

The only other quasi-logical Equilateral Triangle that can be formed (or superimposed) upon/within the schematic is a non-inverted Equilateral Triangle where its base forms between the man's heels while in the X bodily position, whilst the tip of this Equilateral Triangle is found within the man's groin area. However, this Equilateral Triangle is not drawn in large-form—proposed as a necessary element to match the large-form condition of the Square and Circle already drawn within the schematic—and this Equilateral Triangle does not match the *inverted* state of such a conditioned Equilateral Triangle that Da Vinci shaded to surround the man's left eye.

The theory proposes that the *archetype geometric shape* of the Equilateral Triangle (or that of the Tetrahedron in 3D form) represents the *patterned behavioural shape* of a left hemisphere of brain while so extremely (to the highest degree of measure) electrochemically imbalanced (or so extremely isolated away from the counterbalancing/ tempering electrochemical affects of/associated to the right hemisphere), whereby such a brain—within such an electrochemical state, shape, or pattern—is assumed to be solely (practically) of what inevitably somehow mentally transmutes into impulses, sensations, or feelings associated to EXTREME SELFISHNESS that potentially incessantly call upon one's Self to accumulate, hog, or hoard, maximum amounts of possessions and perceived positions-of-power.

NOTE: that such cases are proposed to invariably result in the development and formation of psychological (or behavioural) conditions (or disorders) theorized as being within the mental jurisdiction of a megalomaniac's cold calculation (of quasi-computerized senses of true compassion for others) conducive to cognitive arenas where the ends justify the means

Within such arenas, an individual may be ultimately led by a general perspective where they could fantastically figure to have the entire physical world so accurately (or resolutely) determined—whereat anything observed (or perceived) could possibly be interpreted as wondrously (or irrationally) subject to their mental (or physical) control—that, as per such a proposed premise, such an extremely self-convincing individual may've fallen to such a high degree of *Triangulation of Brain and Perspective* (if you will) that they thereby become much more likely to get enticed, entrapped, or captured by *fierce self-servicing seductions of absolutist temptation* (discussed below) to grossly capitulate toward excessively left hemispheric, *nondual* (or excessively unbalanced), electrochemical aligning (consciously or otherwise) as per the shape, form, or condition of one's mentality.

Such isolated Dark impulses (or such *"fierce self-servicing seductions of absolutist temptation"*)—as proposed to be solely associated to left hemispheric electrochemistry— are theorized to relate to a sort of devilish pull towards lower consciousness, and directly connected to why Leonardo da Vinci drew Vitruvian Man's LEFT EYE to look noticeably DARKER than his right eye, and for why the shape of an Equilateral Triangle is shaded to surround his left eye; while Da Vinci presented all such related messaging representatively (or correspondingly) in front of his LEFT HEMISPERE of his brain.

Conversely, the theory proposes that the *archetype geometric shape* of the Circle (or that of the Sphere in 3D form) represents the *patterned behavioural shape* of a right hemisphere of brain while so extremely (to the highest degree of measure) electrochemically imbalanced (or extremely isolated away from the counterbalancing/offsetting electrochemical affects of/associated to the left hemisphere), whereby such a brain—within such an electrochemical state, shape, or pattern—is assumed to be solely (practically) of what inevitably somehow mentally transmutes into impulses, sensations, or feelings associated to EXTREME SELFLESSNESS that may seem of an incessant calling upon one's Self to abandon all emotional possessions-of-attachment towards anything within the physical realm.

In such a case where a right hemisphere is so extremely isolated electrochemically, the proposed resultant overall psychological state, shape, or condition, is theorized to be of a mental lead where such extreme selfless sensations (or feelings) are experienced, possibly to such a high degree, that the physical world may dramatically cease to make the same rational sense as perhaps it had once before; while as much can involve a seeming irrational extreme wanting (or an imbalanced compulsion) to give away (or to simply abandon) all personal possessions and attachments.

All such proposals (as per the theory) associated to the right hemisphere are considered to somehow relate to why Leonardo da Vinci drew Vitruvian Man's RIGHT EYE to look noticeably more ENLIGHTENED in comparison with the relative Darkness he drew within the look of his left eye, and for why a more Circular shape is shaded to surround his right eye; while Da Vinci presented all such related messaging representatively (or correspondingly) in front of his RIGHT HEMISPHERE of brain; lest we forget that Leonardo set his head to tilt toward the right half (or hemisphere) of the vertically-dissected circle within the schematic.

Within a motif of *dual comparative analysis* concerning the *archetype geometric shapes* of the Equilateral Triangle and the Circle, offered is the contention that more Circular forms of shape naturally (historically) have been associated to:

- the Eternalism (within Buddhist parlance) associated to/of The Creator
- the *Metaphysics* (term defined in Chapter 1) associated to an envisioned pursuit of higher

consciousness; at least generally more attributable toward as much

- the *Sacred Geometry* (term defined in Chapter 4) associated to how angelic images, and such related ideations, somehow have historically been linked to the Circular shape of the halo, and how as much relates to the idea of a human aura

While, conversely, the *archetype geometric shape* of the Equilateral Triangle has long been associable to:

- symbology and imagery linked to concepts of temporal *power gods*
- so-called 'Illuminati' meaning, messaging, or devises
- worldly power structures and systems wherein selfishness trumps selflessness; whereby the impression of being selfless may be considered more of a social tool that could later be parlayed into increasing gains for Self (of actions manifested consciously or otherwise); proposed to be of the Hermetic way, as per such gonzo elitist doctrine

As the book here seems to be winding itself up, a proposal is offered within attempts to perhaps amend an ole mislabelling or sorts.

Within said attempt, it is proposed that in labelling the respective associations of the Left and Right hemispheres, of any given human brain, as definitively Male and Female in nature, essence, or function, that such an approach toward such labelling (or categorizing) may be excessively flawed in terms of *dual analysis*. The main reason for such criticism has directly to do with appreciating the fact that the Right hemisphere of a brain—below the brainstem—physiologically (or operatively) connects to the left half of the body [including all related dynamics (or faculty) of the human heart] whereas both Males and Females have extensively (historically) proven to show great heart in action and behaviour.

The theory contends that the mental (geometrically patterned) shape, state, or condition of Elitism manifests (at least in part) due to excessive degrees of left hemispheric electrochemical dominance (within a brain) over as much associated to that of the right hemisphere; whereby the higher the degree of such left hemispheric electrochemical dominion—domineering over its potentially counterbalancing (or tempering) *dual compadre* in the right hemisphere—then the more extreme (or *nondual*) the imbalance can be within such a shape, state, or condition, thereby the higher the degree of Elitism that can be conditioned (or instilled) within.

As much is offered while appreciating that Leonardo da Vinci was documented to have spent much time around—if not studying within—such elitist social-engineering groups that essentially controlled much of what occurred politically, and culturally, within Renaissance Florence and Venice; whilst some such groups are considered to have been Da Vinci's time-to-time employer (or patron).

As a result, Leonardo is proposed to have most likely learned firsthand of what sort of Dark mental, psychological, or cerebral affects (and effects) that excessive Elitism can have affectively (or effectively) within (or upon) an individual, or how as much could relate to others…namely himself?

Proposed as particularly associative to the above narrative is the relatively common knowledge that Leonardo cryptically wrote—in a note within the margins of his journal, only discovered upon his passing—of the personal affect, and effect, such Medici imposition of sway may've *dually* impressed upon him.

Such a privately recorded comment is proposed to exist as per DaVinci's personal *dual narrative* regarding how the Medici institution is understood to have effectively helped fund, build up, and promote Leonardo's image within the public sphere, while also interpreting (such cryptically written comment) to possibly reveal that Leonardo, through such experience over time, somehow became significant psychologically injured (or Darkly affected) along the way; while determining what actually happened may be more of the mystery.

Perhaps it would be anyone's guess as to which Medici polarity-of-action rubbed off on Leonardo to a more significant (or impactful) degree: The Effective Building? or, The Destructive Affect?
https://www.azquotes.com/quote/654697

The theory suggests that by Leonardo da Vinci drawing Vitruvian Man's head tilting towards the right hemisphere of the vertically-dissected circle that he, thereby, was encoding an intended message subtly (or cryptically) advising his hope for humanity (upon any sort of message discovery) to consciously oversee the development and formation of the state, shape, or condition of our respective patterned electrochemistry— by however slight the majority amount—to error overall toward being more of right hemispheric dominance (over as much associated to that of the left hemisphere) concerning the self-study of *Mentalism* (term defined in Chapter 1).

Perhaps he thought the world could ultimately become a better place, somehow, if more people shared his proposed perspective.

And perhaps, while he was physically alive, Leonardo did not publicly reveal such a perspective due to excessive fear that the Medici would hasten his complete destruction if he had chosen otherwise.

ABOUT THE AUTHOR

Palibor Iversune considers himself a citizen of earth while keeping a national passport. He thinks racism is ridiculous yet carries Human pride. Palibor never authored a book before, but somehow it seemed to write itself. If his character reveals paradox, then the 'culprit' may be cosmic duality of force. He ultimately believes in an ideal of the One love.

CPSIA information can be obtained
at www.ICGtesting.com
Printed in the USA
BVHW051214111022
649147BV00002BA/326